DANCING
IN THE
MOSQUE

HOMEIRA QADERI

TRANSLATED BY ZAMAN STANIZAI

*An Afghan Mother's Letter
to Her Son*

4th ESTATE • London

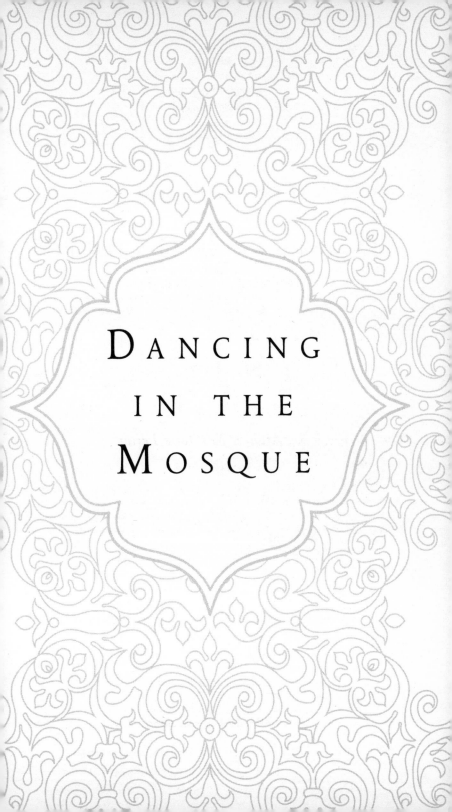

DANCING IN THE MOSQUE

4th Estate
An imprint of HarperCollins*Publishers*
1 London Bridge Street
London SE1 9GF

www.4thEstate.co.uk

First published in Great Britain in 2021 by 4th Estate

First published in the United States by Harper, an imprint of HarperCollins
Publishers, in 2020

1

A catalogue record for this book is available from the British Library

ISBN 978-0-00-837527-0 (hardback)
ISBN 978-0-00-837528-7 (trade paperback)

Designed by Elina Cohen
Ornamental art by Shutterstock / Anna Poguliaeva

Printed and bound in Great Britain by CPI Group (UK) Ltd, Croydon CR0 4YY

To those who value and respect equality

Author's Note

This is a work of nonfiction. The events and experiences detailed herein are all true and have been faithfully rendered as I have remembered them, to the best of my ability. Some names, places, identifying details, and circumstances have been changed in order to protect the privacy and/or anonymity of the various individuals involved.

DANCING

IN THE

MOSQUE

Once upon a time, when there lived a Merciful God, behind the mountains in a distant city a family was given a son with the nickname Shah-Pesar, "One of Regal Descent." His real name was Mushtaq. Shah-Pesar was very handsome. He was his family's lucky charm. One day, to escape his boredom, the family's lucky charm began rummaging through his granny's storage closet. Shah-Pesar didn't know what he was looking for, but something drew him deeper into the dark, dusty interior. Suddenly, his hand closed on a heavy object. It was an old metal lamp.

No sooner had he wiped the hem of his sleeve across the lamp's smooth surface than it became unbearably heavy and sparks shot out of its spout. Astonished, Shah-Pesar dropped the lamp. It hit the floor with a dull thud, rolled around in a circle, and stopped.

A thick coil of smoke rose from the spout, curling toward the ceiling. A pair of stout legs materialized from the smoke, followed by a large belly, a barrel chest, muscular arms, and a huge head. The giant had a black beard topped with curly black hair. His black eyes glowed beneath heavy black eyebrows and a golden earring dangled from his left earlobe, almost touching his shoulder.

Looking down at the trembling boy, the jinni bent down on one knee, and said, "Hello, Master Mushtaq, I am at your service."

Shah-Pesar took a quick step backward and said in a quivering voice, "Why at my service?"

"Because you are the Shah-Pesar of the family," the jinni said. "Your wish is my command."

"What kind of wish?"

"I am the king of all the jinnis. I am powerful enough to grant you anything you desire. I can take you anywhere you wish to go in the blink of an eye or bring you anything you wish just as quickly."

"Bring me a black horse with a long mane and a gleaming coat."

The jinni of the lamp bowed at the knee.

"And a strong hunting bow and eagle-feathered arrows," Shah-Pesar added.

The jinni spun around three times, then three times more. Clapping his hands, he shouted, "Oh, the long-maned black horse of the gleaming coat, appear from the darkness! Master Mushtaq wants to have fun and go hunting."

A cloud of smoke enveloped the middle of the room and turned into a black horse with a full mane and a long, graceful tail. The horse held a hunting bow in its mouth. Bowing down, the horse of the gleaming coat placed the bow at Shah-Pesar's feet and said, "I am all yours, Master Mushtaq."

Dear son,

My grandmother, Nanah-jan, never told me stories like that. In the stories she saved for me, there were no jinnis or magic wands to make my dreams come true. My stories were populated with wild monsters like Baba Ghor-ghori, Barzanghi, Mard-azma, Dokhtar-khor, and hundreds more. My grandmother had more monster stories than beads on her tasbeh. *The purpose of her stories was primarily to keep me from playing with boys, cutting my hair, wearing short skirts, climbing trees, talking to the neighbor girl over the wall, laughing out loud, and ever arguing with Nanah-jan. If I did any of those forbidden things, she would tell me: A monster will appear out of thin air and drag me off to some horrible place where he will eat my flesh and lick my bones, or worse, make me his wife and force me to bear a brood of little hateful ogres.*

My grandmother believed that one of the most difficult tasks that the Almighty can assign anyone is being a girl in Afghanistan. As a child, I didn't want to be a girl. I didn't even want my dolls to be women. In those days, apparently, I knew more ways that led to hell than streets that led to my house. Nanah-jan had told me so many stories about hell that I could describe every neighborhood in hell with my eyes closed. Which is why, when you were born, I was finally accepted and acceptable. At least I had done my duty: I was a mother in this tortured land, and I had produced a son—you, my dearest.

But my motherhood didn't last long. I lost you early on, to the cursed laws of the city, when you were still a breast-feeding nineteen-month-old baby.

It has been 985 nights since you were taken from me. It has been 985 nights since the howling wind wolves have ripped through my lullabies. Now that I am thousands of miles away from you, from all of you, in this small room in California, the only mark of the joy of your birth is the scar gracing my abdomen. It is my badge of motherhood.

I heard that they've asked you about your mother and that you cried when told that your mother is dead. Do not believe them! I haven't died. I am living a life of exile, in a place that has its own beauty, its own laws, and its own problems. But to my eternal pain, it does not have the most important element of my being, of my soul. It does not have you.

1

Bread and Bullets

Afghanistan is the land of invisible bullets and the land of a death foretold, the land of doomed destinies, and the land of dejected and disgruntled youth, waiting forever for dreams that will never come true. This is how *Madar*, my mother, Ansari, and *Nanah-jan*, my grandmother, Firozah, described my homeland to me when I was barely four years old. In their eyes, Afghanistan was divided between the Russian occupiers and their communist government allies on the one side and the mujahideen on the other. But for me, Afghanistan was divided between the street in front of our house where I played during cease-fires, and the dangerous world beyond our walls when war returned and kept me stuck inside.

I was a bright, playful child, too young and energetic to understand fear, whether of invisible bullets buzzing through the air or of Russian tanks rumbling in the street outside our house. Inside those walls, there was a courtyard filled with apple and mulberry trees, and red and green grapes growing on the vine. We were three generations living there: *Baba-jan* and *Nanah-jan*, their four daughters, my aunts Kurbra, Hajar, Zahra, and Azizah, my uncles Naseer and Basheer, *Agha* and *Madar*, plus my baby brother, Mushtaq, and me.

Nanah-jan always said, "A girl should have fear in her eyes."

I spent a lot of time in front of the hallway mirror, examining my eyes to discover where the fear was hiding.

Aunt Zahra told me, "A girl's fear is right on her eyelids."

I would turn my eyelids inside out, hoping to detect the shape or color of fear.

Madar often said, "The night this girl was born, we were surrounded by fire. It felt like the city was giving birth. Before Homeira heard her own cries, she heard other people's screams. No wonder she isn't afraid of anything."

Zahra was seventeen when she was struck by one of those invisible bullets while she was trying to pull me out of the grapevine and carry me to safety in the basement. My poor aunt fell down on her face. I could hear her gasping for breath. Blood was pouring out of her eyes. I stopped searching for the kittens and tried to find the invisible bullet in her eye, the place where a girl's fear is hidden.

I can't remember a time when my homeland was not at war. My childhood began with jet-fighter attacks, bombs falling from the sky, and me trying to count invisible bullets. War and hunger, those are my earliest memories. I remember *Madar* trying to breast-feed my brother, even after he was past the age of two, because there was no food left to eat. Mushtaq chewed and bit my mother's breast. I heard *Madar*'s quiet whimpering when she knew she had no milk left.

During each attack I watched *Nanah-jan* tie her hijab tighter so that she wouldn't die without her veil and be thrown into hell in the hereafter. Even though she was illiterate, she often pretended to read the Holy Qur'an as she would run her index finger over the written lines of the scripture. She wanted to die a Muslim, holding the Holy Book close to her chest. And when I heard *Baba-jan* reading *Surah Yaseen*, the chapter on God's sovereignty, the Day of Judgment, and a warning to nonbelievers, I knew that another bombing attack was coming.

My childhood world was within the bounds of a small window, low in the wall of our house, and a mother who was always trying to keep me away from that window. She knew bullets could pierce glass. She tried her best to keep me surrounded by four solid cement walls. My mother was like a spider trying to safeguard me within her web. But I was a wild, stubborn baby spider. I kept tearing her web apart to escape. I never tired of the struggle to get outside. I was always looking for a chance to sneak into our walled garden. I wanted to be the first to discover the new bullet holes in the walls. I wanted to be the first one to touch the damaged trees and the burnt timber. To be the first to find the kittens hiding under our grapevine. Finding those invisible bullets was my most secret wish. I asked my mother, "Where do all these invisible bullets come from?"

"Homeira," she said, smoothing my hair, "we cannot see where they come from and we never see where they will go until they strike a tree or a wall or, God forbid, a person."

But there were good days, too. I remember sneaking out of the house with Azizah on a day when there was no shooting. I remember the bright sunshine and the flow of a gentle wind of the season. I sat with my back against the sun-warmed wall of our house, playing in the dust and watching people passing by. I was totally unaware of the Russian tanks approaching on the nearby streets.

During cease-fires, I had the habit of going to the smoldering rubble of the bombed houses to see the new ruins and how the gardens had been laid to waste. I wanted to see the crumbling walls, the broken windows, the smashed closets, and the shattered china.

Once, in one of the houses that had been destroyed three or four days earlier, I saw a Russian soldier with his pants down; he was pressing his hand on the mouth of a neighbor's daughter. From behind the wall I laughed at the Russian soldier's bare bottom. He heard my laughter. He quickly got up, put one hand between his legs, and with his other hand he slapped me on my face until it burned. Then he spat in front of me. The girl used that moment to get up, put on her head scarf, and run away through the ruins.

Later I would laughingly tell everyone this story about how red the Russian soldier's buttocks were. Upon hearing my account of the event, Uncle Basheer punched the wall with his fists in anger. *Baba-jan* didn't laugh at the story. He just wiped his tears.

In those days, Herat was a very strange mixture of heaven and hell. Sometimes, when the city was at peace, you could hear the returning birds chirping in trees. Sometimes, I could hear sweet musical notes as our neighbor's son, Shuaib, sat on the wall playing a reed flute. I would dance to his music on our terrace, but *Nanah-jan* feared that melody, believing that the sound of the flute foretold early death. And soon, indeed, Shuaib died in a fire that consumed his house.

Nanah-jan once said, "I wish we were all birds, so we could fly out of this place."

Almost every morning there was a long row of olive-green Russian tanks on the street in front of the hospital near our house, their engines idling under the tall pine trees that lined the road in a cacophony of noise. They would disappear in the haze of dusk. I asked my grandfather, "*Baba-jan*, tell me, where do the tanks come from every morning and where do they go every night?"

Baba-jan looked and whispered under his breath, "They come from hell and they go back to hell."

I told Azizah that we should follow behind the Russian tanks so we could discover the path to hell.

"It's too far away, Homeira," she said emphatically. "We would get very tired."

I told her she was afraid of the Russian tanks.

When *Nanah-jan* no longer had nuts in her pockets, she could no longer bribe Azizah and me to stay in the house. As soon as the city lapsed into silence, we would escape into the street when *Madar* and *Nanah-jan* weren't looking. Once, a soldier gave me a tin of canned food. Because we were always hungry, I brought it home. *Nanah-jan* was horrified, shouting, "Ḥarām! Ḥarām! These cans are filled with frogs," she said. "That's what the red soldiers eat."

When Azizah and I heard this, we ran into the backyard and threw up.

A few frogs lived in the small stream in our garden, jumping around during the day and croaking their special songs in the evening. On the nights when there was silence, my heart broke for those poor little frogs. I knew the Russians had eaten them. I cried for them under my blanket.

During the cease-fires, our entertainment was collecting pinecones or running among the tanks, playing hide-and-seek with the boys. When the boys hid and I couldn't find them, the Russian soldiers sitting on the tank turrets would point to the boys' hiding spots. I remember that whenever I found a boy, the soldiers would clap and shout, their faces growing red with their laughter. Then I understood why we called the Soviet Army the "Red Army."

One day, when it was my turn to hide, one of those red soldiers beckoned me over, a big smile on his round face. He bent down from the top of the tank, reaching his arms toward me. I held my arms up to him. He took my hands and pulled me up into the tank, scraping my shoulder against its hot iron side. My shoulder hurt, but I forgot the pain as soon as I looked around. I stared in amazement at the hundreds of buttons and blinking lights. It was stuffy inside and very hot. Another soldier was sitting on a metal seat. When he caught sight of me, he leaned toward me and said something to the first soldier, who answered quickly. They both started laughing. Then the seated man put his face against a round object.

I crawled over and began to touch some buttons beside him. Looking at me over his shoulder, he said, "*Nyet. Na, na.*"

I pointed at the tube. He leaned back in his seat and motioned for me to stand in front of him. I put my eye against the end of the tube. Inside I saw a small, round city. When the soldier turned a knob, the city became smaller. He turned the knob more, and the city inside became tiny and far away. I got scared and pulled my eye away. I looked around. We were all still the same size inside the tank. The soldier laughed and turned the knob again. He gestured with his chin, asking me to look into the tube again. The city came closer. The trees got bigger. The size of people standing and crying in front of the hospital grew larger. I saw Azizah, who was still looking for me. Her face was big enough in the tube to see the fear in her eyes. I saw girls in flowery dresses collecting pinecones. The boys had lost the game; they couldn't find me.

I was five when I saw my city from inside the viewfinder of a Russian tank, my small city, my big city, the city that was very far from me and yet very close to me again. The soldier gave me chocolate. I looked at him and felt ashamed.

On one of those days, one of those tanks fired at our neighborhood and left half of our street in ruins. Another hit our grapevine. We then went to the basement and were living there for a while. We covered the floor with two large rugs and brought down blankets and slept there at night.

I played for hours with a doll that *Nanah-jan* had made for me. I asked *Nanah-jan*, "Can you make another dress for my doll so she becomes happy again?"

Nanah-jan promised that she would, as soon as she found some nice fabric.

So I was overjoyed when the tailor shop down the street took a direct hit. As soon as the jets disappeared from the sky, I ran outside and searched the ruins for some beautiful cloth for my doll. Rummaging through the debris, I found a few nice pieces that were only a little dusty.

I ran home and showed them to *Nanah-jan*. I was so excited about getting a new dress made for my doll that I forgot to tell her I saw a hand moving in the rubble. My grandmother looked at the fabric and her eyes widened. "Take it back! This is *ḥarām*!"

"These aren't frogs!" I said.

I never gave them back to the moving hand. I hid them under the grapevine.

During the war, there was no flour, so *Nanah-jan* couldn't bake bread anymore, not even the usual two small cakes for Azizah and me. It got even worse later when the roads to Herat were all blocked by the fighting and we didn't even have potatoes to eat.

Nanah-jan said that the mujahideen were starving as well.

"They can eat frogs," I said. "Or those big Russian chocolates with honey inside."

"Homeira," a startled *Nanah-jan* said. "How do you know what's inside Russian chocolate?"

In an attempt to survive the Russian onslaught, people had learned how to pretend to be sympathetic to Russians by hoisting red banners on their front doors or roofs. Aunt Hajar hung a bright red cloth from the clothesline in the yard, so when the Russian jets were spinning above they would see our household as being sympathetic to them and wouldn't bomb us. My grandmother, who considered any sympathy with the communists a sin, cursed her, saying we would all die as *kaffirs*, nonbelievers, and end up in hell. "We are not communists! Take down that red cloth from the clothesline," she said.

"Does being a Muslim or a *kaffir* depend on a red cloth? She considers the hoisting of the red cloth an act of blasphemy and doesn't understand these murderous Russians. Does she really think God is that unmerciful?" Hajar said. "I just don't want to be killed."

At night, it was the mujahideen's turn. They did a house-to-house search for communists and collaborators, climbing walls and jumping into gardens and courtyards. Aunt Hajar hung a green cloth from the clothesline. I teased her, saying, "Should I tell the mujahideen that you hang a red cloth out in the day-time?"

"Homeira! I will tell them you ate Russian chocolate," she said.

I became frightened and ran to my grandmother. "Tell Aunt Hajar not to scare me, *Nanah-jan*."

My aunt laughed and stuck out her tongue.

Uncle Naseer was a mujahid, a resister of the Russian invasion. Mujahideen were labeled rebels by the government, but people liked them and supported them and called them "the defenders of the faith." They fought the Russians and suffered a lot, but they were eventually able to expel the invading Soviet forces from Afghanistan. That's when they were also considered the defenders of the homeland.

Uncle Naseer came and went like a ghost, jumping into our yard after dark and hiding on the roof with his Kalashnikov. I'd hear his footsteps overhead and then hear him land in the yard.

Every night my grandfather took a mattress, a pillow, and blankets up to the roof. He always looked worried when my uncle was nearby. "Where did Uncle go, *Baba-jan*?" "*Hush*, child; he's gone to count the stars."

"Where does he sleep, *Baba-jan*?"

"Uncle Naseer's house is on the moon, Homeira."

"Can one sleep better on the moon, *Baba-jan*?"

Baba-jan sighed. "Yes, Homeira, but you must wake up before the moon sets or it will swallow you."

Every night I watched the moon, worried that if Uncle Naseer overslept, the moon would swallow him.

That very night, agents of KhAD, the State Intelligence Agency, stormed into our house looking for Uncle Naseer. Terrified, I pointed to the roof and said, "Stars! Stars!"

My dear Siawash,

I am sure that someday when you learn that your mother has been alive all these years, you will be angry. You will ask yourself, "How could a mother just walk away and leave her child behind?" It was never my wish.

I wish that neither of us belonged to a society that victimizes mothering and motherhood. I hope that by the time you grow up, this attitude will have changed or disappeared. I, my mother, my mother's mother, and my mother's mother's mother have all spent our lives hoping for that change. Please don't think that my yearning for you and even for your father has left me completely. Not so . . . but I have learned to pay a price for my ambitions. I don't regret the sacrifices I have made, for I know that through this suffering I am, I hope, making a difference for other women, the ones who will come after me.

Trust me and believe in the history that I'm trying to make. Try not to be angry at me for this separation. Instead believe in yourself, for it is you and I together who must create a new Afghanistan. I look forward to the day when the two of us will live in a society of equals. Even from the darkness of this dungeon, I look forward to the day when a blue sky will unfurl its bright and beautiful horizons. Nobody is going to give us this blue sky for free. We must take it by and for ourselves.

2

Migrating Swallows

Every season came and went, but the season of war was endless.

During the seventh summer of the Russian invasion, our half-burnt mulberry tree was heavy with fruit. The sparrows pecked at it, scattering berries across the yard. From behind the window, I pointed to the fallen berries to help the sparrows find them. But they paid no attention. They were fighting with the mynah birds chattering in the branches.

For two nights, the sky was peaceful, filled only with stars and a thin moon. Uncle Basheer came home late, after being out most of the night. "Did you go to the moon with Uncle Naseer?" I asked.

"No, I was standing in front of Wali's window, watching his television. I couldn't hear the sound, but I saw Russian men and women dancing together. And then I saw pictures of our mujahideen who had been killed . . ."

"Uncle Basheer, what is television?" I asked.

"It is a box, and in it you can see lots of different people."

"But, Uncle, how can all those people fit inside a box?"

Nanah-jan called out from across the room, "There are only short people in that box, Homeira."

After dinner, I noticed that Uncle Basheer had disappeared again. I took my shoes and snuck out of the house. I wanted to see that box and see those women dancing inside it.

The veil of night spread darkness over the streets. We were forbidden from going out after dark. *Nanah-jan* had warned us, "When it gets dark, the infidels hunger for blood."

I looked for Uncle Basheer, but I couldn't see him. I looked in both directions, making sure there were no bloodthirsty infidels lurking. *Nanah-jan*'s voice whispered in my ear, "The infidels bite the vein in your neck and suck all the blood out. They like to grab a bunch of children all at once. And they like girls' blood the most, Homeira!"

I heard a man running down the street. I shrank against the wall. Was he one of the bloodthirsty infidels or a neighbor running away from them?

My heart was pounding in my chest. Could the infidels hear it? I didn't want to attract vampires. Hearing the sound of flowing water, I remembered the culvert built into Wali's wall where a stream emptied from his yard into a ditch beside the street. In the fall rains, it was full of water, but now there was only a trickle. I crawled into the culvert.

I covered my mouth with my hand in case a frog would try to jump onto my face. I crawled forward. The culvert opened into a corner of the courtyard. I stood up and looked around. Uncle Basheer was standing in the yard, silhouetted by a window that flickered with a soft blue light. I crept up to him. "Uncle?"

Shocked, my uncle whirled around. "Homeira! What are you doing here?"

"I want to watch television, Uncle."

"You're too short to see in the window. Go home right now!"

I clung to my uncle's leg. "Please, just once! Just once!"

Uncle Basheer looked at me with one eye, while he kept the other glued to the television. A woman's singing reached us from inside the house. My uncle hoisted me onto his shoulders. A gentle breeze wrapped its cool breath around my sweaty neck.

"Careful, Homeira. We don't want Wali's father to see us."

Uncle Basheer raised me to the height of the window. I saw something lit up in the corner of the room. I squinted my eyes . . . I couldn't believe it . . . the woman's voice was coming from that box, a woman with bare legs, wearing a short dress, not trousers. I squeezed Uncle Basheer's neck. The Box Woman looked nothing like *Nanah-jan*. She looked like Samira's mother, a teacher, who walked to school without a hijab, wearing a skirt and a sleeveless blouse.

Suddenly, the night exploded. Stuttering bullets shattered the silence.

Uncle Basheer's friend Wali appeared at the window, placed a finger on his lips, and closed the window. A frightening noise hissed by my ear—a hot breath of wind. I heard glass breaking. Wali was still there, standing at the window, right in front of me, staring right at me, his eyes opening wider and wider. And then, suddenly he fell over.

Watching, my uncle fell to his knees. My face was burning in a hundred places as if I had been stung by a swarm of bees. My hands were wet and sticky. Inside the house, Wali's mother and sister were screaming.

"Uncle?" I asked.

Basheer didn't answer.

I jumped off his shoulders and stared into his eyes. Uncle Basheer was looking at me, his eyes wide and unblinking.

I pulled on his arm. "Let's go home, Uncle."

He stood up. I pulled him toward the culvert. I crawled in; he followed. We slithered under the wall. *Baba-jan*'s voice was calling from down the street.

"We're here, *Baba-jan*!" I shouted.

Baba-jan ran toward us; *Madar* and *Nanah-jan* were right behind him. Uncle Basheer fell down. Lifting him up, *Baba-jan* carried him to our house. Once inside, *Agha* knelt beside me, examining my hands and face. "It's Uncle Basheer's blood," I said. "The bullet passed right next to us. It hit Wali's stomach."

Screaming, Uncle Basheer jumped up and ran toward the door. *Baba-jan* caught him, holding him tightly, while Uncle Basheer screamed and screamed. *Madar* washed my bloody hands and cleaned my face, removing bits of glass with a pair of tweezers. The sky blazed brightly; then fell dark . . . light . . . darkness. I could feel the tanks' rumbling outside.

When I woke up in the morning, Uncle Basheer was sitting in a corner with his face in his hands, crying. I crawled toward him.

"Uncle Basheer, what happened to Wali?"

Uncle Basheer cried louder. My face began to burn again.

Neither my grandfather nor my grandmother went to Wali's

funeral. "They were communists," *Baba-jan* said. "They wouldn't like us reciting *Fâteha* at the funeral."

Crying, Uncle Basheer said, "But Wali wasn't a communist!"

Madar said, "A bullet doesn't care whether you are a mujahid or a communist. The smoke from the fires that started in this country scorches everyone's eyes."

Wali was buried in his yard under a burnt pomegranate tree. They couldn't take him to the cemetery because the streets were packed with both communists and mujahideen.

Baba-jan said to *Agha*, "Wakil Ahmad, take the hands of your wife and children and go. They will come for you next. This land doesn't belong to you or me anymore."

That night, *Baba-jan* wrapped me in his arms. "Come to me, Homeira."

I fell asleep in his arms. I don't remember anything he said, I only remember that he was repeatedly drying his eyes with the tip of his turban.

When I awoke, it was very warm. My mouth was filled with dust. My face was burning. I rolled over and sat up. The blazing sun was directly overhead, shining. I looked around. I was surrounded by a flat, empty desert, without a single shadow—a dun-colored landscape with thorn bushes scattered all the way to an incandescent horizon.

I thought that our house must have been flattened by a rocket; that our entire neighborhood had been destroyed. But there was not even a pile of adobe or a burnt tree branch to be seen.

"Where is *Baba-jan*, Aunt Azizah, *Nanah-jan* . . . ?"

Agha put a finger to his lips. "We are emigrating."

It was my first time hearing this word. I crawled over next to *Madar*. Shading her eyes with one hand, she gazed at the small thorn bushes in the distance. "*Madar*, what does 'emigrating' mean?"

Still searching the horizon, *Madar* said, "It means becoming a stranger in a foreign country. . . . It means dying alone."

I had a thousand questions, but neither of my parents was looking at me. "*Madar*, when we emigrate, can I still sleep next to *Baba-jan*?"

Madar's eyes were fixed on the distant rocky plain lying at the foot of the mountains. The hot wind scoured the soft soil, lifting it high into the air, creating whirling funnels of dust that danced across the landscape.

In the distance, I saw a motorcycle, a tiny speck trailing a huge plume of dust, growing larger and larger, ripping the heart out of the plain with its roaring.

With the two *boghcha* on his shoulder, *Agha* began to run faster. "*Agha!* Why didn't you bring *Baba-jan*?" I ran after him.

Madar was trying to reach us. I shouted, "*Madar*, what happened to *Nanah-jan*?"

The wind threw the sand against my face, filling my mouth with dust. It didn't taste like anything.

The motorcycle reached us. The driver shouted, "Hurry up! Hurry up!"

I raised my arm and waved good-bye at the invisible home. The driver was driving as fast as he could.

The thornbushes flew by, big and small.

I wished I had kissed *Baba-jan's* face before we'd left. I thought to myself, *The wars were not this bad. At least we were all together.*

I decided to count the steps that were taking us farther and farther away from everything I knew. One, two, three . . . Faster! One, two, three . . . One, two.

A year later, in the depths of the winter, after the Russians left Afghanistan, we returned to Herat, eagerly awaiting the return of spring, eagerly awaiting the return of peace. I knew about the seasons, but I didn't know what peace was. For me, it was enough to feel once again surrounded by *Baba-jan's* embrace. It didn't matter what little of the house and the garden remained intact.

My dear Siawash,

The only things I have received from the fourteen years of shared life with your father are a few pictures of you that I've hung on the walls and the door of my room here in California. In the mornings my eyes open to your sweet face and at night my eyes close looking at that same face. Even though you must have grown past the age of breast-feeding, at your nightly feeding hour I still wake up, afraid I may have missed it. I stare at all the pictures of you I have on my wall, but the one I look at most is the picture on your birth certificate. It takes me back to the day this certificate was issued.

On the day after you were born a frigid wind burst

through my open window. Out on the street, people must've been collecting the scattered body parts of their dead relatives. A yellow-orange water tanker had come to help the snow wash away the crimson streaks of human cruelty.

But I didn't want to think about the blood and bodies I had seen the day before. All my thoughts were with you as you were sleeping comfortably in my arms, and looking at your little pink face had taken away all the despair of Kabul from me.

It was eleven thirty in the morning. I heard the coughing of a man behind the curtain of my room. I hurriedly pulled a blanket to cover my bosom. A man dressed in a blue uniform came from behind the curtain and greeted me. He had a pen and a folder that seemed to contain thick yellow cards. The man looked at my mother and me and asked, "Don't you have a man around?" My mother kept quiet, but I replied, "He has stepped outside, but we can talk, too." The man shook his head at my audacity and said, "I'll come back." He had hardly left the room when your father entered. The man introduced himself to your father behind the curtain and said that he had come to fill out the birth certificate of the newborn to complete the record. The man asked your father, "Is the newborn a girl or a boy?" I could hear your father's excitement. "It's a king-boy," he said. The man asked, "His name?" Your father responded, "Siawash." Obviously, the man was filling out those yellow birth certificates behind the curtain.

The man asked for your father's name and then for the name of your father's father. Then he asked for the gynecologist's certification papers. Your father picked up those papers from the table next to the bed and gave them to the man. I could hear him flipping through the papers. Moments later, when the man was done filling out the information, he congratulated your father and left.

You were busy nursing. When your father came through the curtain, he had the yellow birth certificate in his hand. I took the birth certificate from him and read it. It contained your name, your father's name, and your grandfather's name. But nobody had asked for my name. I was irrelevant. I looked at you and I wanted to hide you back in my womb so that once again you could belong to me, too.

I gave the birth certificate to my mother. As she was reading it, she sighed deeply. Although she was clearly upset, she was not surprised; she had lived as a woman in Afghanistan all her life.

Later, when your father brought in the identity registration card, once again my name, as your mother, was nowhere to be seen. Even in your passport, they didn't ask for my name. Your mother's name does not appear in any paper document. My son, in your motherland the mentioning of a woman's name outside the family circle is a source of shame. And no child is known by its mother's name.

But don't worry, dear son. Should you one day want to find your live-buried mother, I have tried to leave you a sign, a clue, a hint. On your birth certificate next to your name, when no one was looking, I wrote in a bright color, "Mother's name: Homeira."

3

The Spinning Gardonah

In February 1989 the Russians left our country. One day heli-
copters were hovering overhead like huge, angry, flying dragons
as we cowered in darkness; the next day, the endless blue sky
was filled with flights of doves, sparrows, and mynahs, testing
their wings after years in hiding. But the chasm between the
Afghan people and the government grew even wider. President
Najibullah was unable to gain the support of mujahideen resistance groups and his government forces continued to fight the
mujahideen, while KhAD and the Islamist factions stalked the
cities, killing their enemies.

Despite Herat's ruined vistas and fallen monuments, life had
started moving through the city's streets like blood pumping
through a resuscitated child's veins. The city took a deep breath.
People began to climb out of their basements, where they had
huddled for years. They could finally stand in the sun beneath
the open sky and speak to each other without having to shout
over the screams of low-flying rockets and jet fighters.

The mujahideen struggled home, the survivors, the wounded, the blind, the lame, the limbless, the foot soldiers. They came to look for their families. Some found orphans, some found homes, others found bone-filled craters where their homes had once stood.

Many people that KhAD arrested never returned, but Uncle Basheer came back. Everything seemed fine, except he was missing some of his fingernails. Whenever I asked him what had happened to them, he hid his hands in his sleeves and said nothing. Uncle Naseer also returned, with only one missing kidney. I never dared ask about that.

Our own house was still standing, but the neighborhood along the river was a wasteland of water-filled bomb craters. Cut down by bombs or for winter firewood, not a single tree remained standing in the *Bagh-e Zananah*, the Women's Garden, which surrounded Queen Goharshad's mosque and mausoleum.

For two years, we held our breath, unaware that this lull would soon be followed by a storm of discord and civil war.

My fondest memories belong to a time after the Russian retreat. In those days, we took short excursions to Kababian village, where I ran in the meadows with no fear of bombs. This village where *Nanah-jan* had spent her childhood was a place I could let my mind roam free in childhood fantasies. We went twice each year, once during the mulberry season and again in the fall when the wheat was cut and threshed.

When the mulberries were ripe, I would spend all day up among their leafy branches, picking the ripe red and milk-white mulberries. The sparrows were my rivals, stealing my harvest. I ate my fill before the birds arrived. Except sometimes it was the other way around.

The women spread their shawls beneath the trees. We children would climb like monkeys, kicking and shaking the branches, so the mulberries would fall like purple and white snow in the scarves stretched to collect them below.

Women would put the collected mulberries in baskets that were then lowered in the clear flowing stream so the water would cool them.

Afterward, the village women sat in the shade, leaning their heads together and gossiping while they ate the cool, ripe berries and *doogh*, a yogurt drink. And I hid in the branches above them, eavesdropping on their small talk and chirping with the sparrows.

Once in a while, *Madar* would call me. "Sparrow, come down now."

"*Madar*, the sparrows are protesting. They are complaining that we have picked all the ripe berries and left nothing for them."

"Homeira, tell the sparrows to stop complaining. They have wings and can fly from tree to tree, wherever their desires take them. Tell them, child, that the sun is shining and will soon ripen more berries for them."

I tried to explain to the birds exactly what *Madar* had told me, but they just chirped their protests and blinked their beady eyes at me. "*Madar!*" I said. "I understand what they are saying. I just can't speak to them."

Madar's laughter rose among the shiny leaves. "Understanding them is not enough, my daughter. You should be able to speak to them as well."

My six-year-old brother Mushtaq chimed in, "Yes, Homeira, you must be able to speak to the birds. *Everyone* knows what they are saying."

"And *you* know how to speak to them, I suppose?" I said to him in astonishment.

"Yes, look," Mushtaq said. He took off his shoe and threw it up into the branches. The sparrows exploded into the sky in a noisy cloud. "*That's* how you speak to them!"

In *Nanah-jan*'s village, my favorite pastime was to slip away in the heat of the afternoon and explore the narrow streets. I believed that one of those narrow streets would turn a corner and I would suddenly end up in the round part of the earth.

Madar told me that the world was divided between light and darkness, the night on one side and day on the other. One day I searched and searched that labyrinth of streets to find an alley where one half was in darkness and the other half in light.

Pale and out of breath, I finally reached home just as the crescent moon was suspended above the high walls of the compound.

"I was searching for the other end of the world, *Madar-jan*."

The best part of my visits to the village was riding the *gardonah*, the wheat-threshing wooden chassis hauled around in circles by a team of oxen over wheat sheaves spread on a floor of rammed earth. As the *gardonah* circled around, loosening the wheat hulls away from the harder kernels, we kids sat on the *gardonah* as it went around and round, our weight helping to thresh the grain. I always managed to find a place on the *gardonah* with the older children.

When the wind was blowing, the chaff from under the thresh-ing floor and the *gardonah* would rise in a dusty cloud, cover-ing my face and hair. In excitement, I would burst into joyous screams. I wished that when the spinning of the *gardonah* came to an end, I would open my eyes on the other side of the world. My mother was always complaining about me and watched me closely. She would say, "You are a lot of trouble, Homeira. Why aren't you like the other village girls? Why must you always be in the very middle of things?"

Like my brother, I was a rebel, but a very different kind. *Madar* and *Nanah-jan* usually approved of his mischief. Even when he broke *Nanah-jan*'s winter bedroom window. Or when he would displace the broken clay pitcher that *Nanah-jan* had placed in the tree for the sparrows to nest in. He would say, "Let the birds struggle to find their eggs." *Nanah-jan* would even tol-erate Mushtaq playing with her prayer beads, using them as a harness around my neck. He would kick me saying, "Hey, lazy horse, move it." And when I would free myself from his harness screaming and shouting, *Nanah-jan* would say, "It wouldn't kill you if you let your brother play with you as his horse. He is much younger than you." And when that same younger brother would eventually become bigger than both my sister, Zahra, who was named after my aunt, and me, he would be given a bigger share of meat at dinner. When I would say to *Nanah-jan*, "I want the same size piece as Mushtaq," she would look at me and say, "Since when has a girl's share become equal to a boy's?"

This kind of double-standard treatment infuriated me and

led me to break rules. Even though I was a girl, I would walk swiftly and even run around the courtyard. I got a great kick out of the fact that I was able to climb a tree and *Nanah-jan* couldn't climb after me to pull me down. I had learned to climb up the tree very quickly and would do everything possible to make sure I climbed a higher branch than Mushtaq. I remember always trying to climb the highest branches, and then one day I fell down from the tree. *Nanah-jan* shook her head with some gratification and said, "It was God's doing."

I was crying. *Madar* lifted me up from the dusty ground. My knees were bloody and bruised. *Madar* said, "May God keep your destiny in safe hands. You always do things you are not supposed to."

Nanah-jan said, "In ancient times they would chain a girl's feet together so that she wouldn't stride wider and wouldn't become a source of shame for her family."

I was never concerned about the chain on the feet or the family honor. I didn't even understand what that meant. I was in my own world. Away from the eyes of my grandfather, my uncles, and my father, I would spend half the day climbing the walls with Zarghuna, the neighbor's daughter. Whenever we would hear a knock on the front door of either house, we would jump from the wall down to the veranda. With Shakiba, our other neighbor's daughter, we would polish our nails and hold our hands in the sun to dry. We would enjoy the sunshine on our light skin. We did this in spite of *Nanah-jan*'s frequent nagging that this was the behavior of girls destined for hellfire. I would convince Mahjabin, another neighbor's daughter, to play seesaw with me. We would ride timbered logs that would definitely bring shame to the past seven generations of a girl's family and stain the honor of the mothers in any household. Years later, when Mahjabin was rejected and returned to her family by her husband because her virginity wasn't intact, *Nanah-jan* fainted by the side of the wall and said, "May God save the destiny of this other log rider."

In those days I committed my own sins and led the neighborhood girls to commit theirs. Especially on days when we couldn't reach the raw grapes on the trellis. I would persuade the other girls to hold the bricks and climb like cats so our hands could reach the raw grapes that we loved so much. Mushtaq called me "the frightening creeper climber."

"You have a thousand feet, but you won't be able to step outside of the four walls of this house," he would say.

I remember when he was not quite a teenager, I said to him, "I would leave the house even if I didn't have feet to walk on."

He said, "Where would you go?"

I said, "To the other side of the world, far away from you."

We loved each other even though my share of the meat never became the same size as his.

My reputation as a troublemaker lives on, even all these years and miles away. It was just the other day that Mushtaq messaged me: You always wanted to be on the other side of the planet. Now that you are there, are you happy? Is there anything else you are wishing for?

I sent him a message in return: I wish there was a magic gardo-nah that I could ride on and it would spin and spin until I am on your side of the world once again.

He wrote back immediately: Girl, you need to settle down in one place. One day, with all this spinning around and around, you will become so dizzy that you will lose yourself altogether.

My little Siawash,

As I am thousands of miles away from you, and your father doesn't even let me talk to you on the phone or through a video call, I begged my mother to go to Kabul four months ago to see you and represent me in the courtroom. For going to such a place is taboo. She doesn't like to walk in the hallways among people who condemn women, always, as guilty. If the ignominy of her daughter's divorce wasn't bad enough, she now has to endure further suffering in these courts of shame. But Madar *entered this realm of injustice without hesitation, on my behalf, and on behalf of motherhood.*

At two thirty in the morning in California, I heard the court verdict on the phone line with my own ears. The judge said in a commanding voice:

"This woman is no longer a mother. There is no need for the mother and child to know each other."

I couldn't cry any louder. My anger shredded my heart into pieces. Is it even possible for a mother to forget her child?

Siawash,

No scrap of paper will ever be able to forbid me to love you.

I told Madar *to return to Herat. She did all she could—not just for her daughter, but for her daughter's motherhood as well.*

4

Hush—Silence!

There were plenty of happier days in those early postwar years, too. Days in which I sat by the river, my hair gathered into two fluffy ponytails, eating a big piece of *naan* without needing to save any for Mushtaq. Older kids played hide-and-seek among the ruined houses, running across the roofs as night fell. For a child who had seen nothing but war and darkness, Herat was suddenly extravagant and spectacular.

Once the Russians were gone, families began to send their children back to school to catch up on the lost years of their education. Never mind that the schools were piles of rubble, the tombs of thousands of children. If they had gates, they lacked walls. If they had walls, they didn't have windows. Tents were set up in the school yards, steamy saunas under the blazing sun.

I was still young enough to run carefree through the streets, playing my loud games. It was still no one's business where I went or when I came back. I had escaped from the dark basement with its spiderwebs and unseen thunder overhead; that was all that mattered.

Both in times of peace and times of war, reading the Qur'an has always been more important than a general education in Afghanistan, especially for girls. At a very young age, children are taken to the mosque so that a mullah can teach them Qur'an. Even if a girl couldn't attend school, she had to study Qur'an. There were no exceptions

When my sister, Zahra, was in first grade, my grandparents insisted that after her daily studies at Mehri Herawi High School, Zahra attend the mosque in the afternoons in order to study Qur'an from Maulawi Rashid.

On Zahra's first day, *Nanah-jan* wrapped a dozen sugared almonds in a handkerchief and walked us to the mosque. It was late afternoon and the shadows were creeping up the walls. A gentle breeze shook the leaves of the mulberry trees along the river. Holding hands, Zahra and I walked along behind *Nanah-jan*, as carefree as sparrows.

When we entered the mosque, the maulawi was sitting in a corner, while the children sat before him in the courtyard holding their Qur'ans on their laps. The afternoon wind circled the walls, lifting the girls' scarves, ruffling their hair, and fluttering the pages of their sacred texts. The girls struggled to keep their hijabs from blowing off with one hand while they held their Qur'ans open with the other. The air was heavy with the scent of jasmine blooming along the walls.

Nanah-jan greeted Maulawi Rashid. "I am from the family of Haji Sahib Faqir Ahmad Khan. I would like to have my granddaughter begin her studies here."

Staring at me, the maulawi scratched his beard. "But she is all grown up!"

Nanah-jan pushed Zahra forward. "It's already too late for my eldest granddaughter, but I brought her younger sister."

Zahra's hijab had fallen to her shoulders, revealing her light brown hair and exposing her light complexion in the sunlight. The maulawi frowned. "Girl, why aren't you wearing your shawl properly? A hijab is for covering your hair, not your neck."

Zahra hid behind *Nanah-jan*. The maulawi pointed at me. "That one is a woman. She needs to be taken care of. Next time she comes, make sure she wears a dress with long sleeves."

Nanah-jan gave the maulawi her handkerchief full of *noqol*. "Yes, Maulawi *Sahib*. When can Zahra begin her lessons?"

"She can start today," he said, never taking his eyes off me. His eyes crawled over my body while his words were directed to *Nanah-jan*.

Nanah-jan smiled, tears welling up under her burqa. "God bless you, Maulawi *Sahib*."

"Learning the Qur'an isn't important for *that* one," the maulawi said, lifting his chin in my direction while his gaze never left my body. "But covering her shame is. Find her a bigger hijab to hide her hair and body. She is, what, eleven or twelve? Her breasts are beginning to show."

Nanah-jan nagged me all the way home. "Homeira, you will ruin our family's honor."

But I wasn't listening. I was thinking about the maulawi's staring eyes.

A month had passed since Zahra and Mushtaq had enrolled at the mosque. One Thursday *Nanah-jan* asked me to bring her water from the river for her ablutions. It was noon, the streets were empty, the shadows had disappeared beneath the walls.

When I reached the river, the maulawi was standing in the water, his pants around his knees. I hesitated for a few seconds, then knelt on the riverbank and bent down to dip the *aftabah*, the pitcher, in the water. I watched the water filling it up, *gohloob, gohloob, gohloob*.

Suddenly I heard *hush*—a very quiet *hush*, like a bird settling on a branch in springtime or the wind blowing through mulberry leaves. *Hush*. A fish blowing bubbles from deep in the river.

Hush.

I looked up. It wasn't a bird. It wasn't the wind. It wasn't a fish beneath the river. The maulawi was trying to get my attention:

Hush.

He'd tucked his shirt beneath his chin. His pants were around his knees. His hand was between his legs, rubbing himself.

Staring straight at me, the maulawi rubbed himself, grunting and sighing.

I turned to run away. My feet slipped out beneath me. I fell into the water. The red plastic pitcher dropped from my hands and sank. My sodden dress stuck to my body.

Hush.

Trembling with fear, I scrambled up the riverbank. My mind was filled with the image of that thing between the maulawi's legs. I ran home, leaving a dark trail of water in the dusty alley. *Nanah-jan* was sitting in the yard next to our garden. "Where's my water? What happened to my pitcher? Can't a twelve-year-old do anything right these days?"

I didn't reply. I collapsed in a corner. Still shaking, I leaned my head on my knees. I was a small branch bent by the horror of an ugly wind.

Nanah-jan sent Mushtaq to search for the *aftabah*, but he never found it.

I hid from *Nanah-jan* every time I heard the *adhan*. I never wanted to go to the river for her.

One day, Zahra came down with a high fever. *Madar* said that she should stay home from school and mosque, but studious Zahra didn't want to miss even one day of class. Coming home at noon, her fever was worse, and her eyes had turned red. She lay down on the rug with her shoes on and slept for an hour. When she woke up, *Madar* gave her some medicine and fed her a bowl of lamb soup. "You must rest this afternoon, dear. If you don't feel better by tomorrow, you shouldn't go to school then either."

Dropping her head onto her pillow, Zahra slept. *Madar* went out to bake bread. Engrossed in my reading, I forgot completely about my sister. "Homeira, where's Zahra?" *Madar* asked when she returned to the living room.

Zahra was gone. We searched the whole house. Her Qur'an was missing as well. "She must have gone to the mosque," *Madar* said. "She is always afraid of being whipped for missing class." *Madar* covered my hair with my hijab. "Go! Bring your sister back; she is too sick to be going anywhere."

I didn't want to face that maulawi, but I had no choice. *Madar* blamed me for not watching Zahra; I had to go after her.

Stupid girl! I said to myself. *This was the wrong time to burrow your nose in a book.* Wrapping myself in my shawl, I ran down the street, terrified that I would have to speak to the maulawi.

My steps slowed as I neared the mosque. The hot sun was heavy on my head. The mosque's courtyard was empty. There was no one around to help me. The maulawi had probably taken the children inside because of the heat. Wrapping my shawl tighter around my body, I entered the mosque, filled with dread. Inside, I hesitated. I could hear the children chanting *surahs* from farther within, a hubbub of mumbled Arabic. I waited a few minutes by the entrance, gathering my courage. Then I heard Zahra. She was crying. I rushed inside.

The boys were sitting on one side of the mosque, their bodies swaying as they chanted. Mushtaq looked up, surprised to see me. A curtain hung in the middle of the room. Zahra's crying was coming from the other side.

All the boys were staring at me. In a soft voice, I asked where Maulawi *Sahib* was. They pointed to the curtain. Taking a deep breath, I pulled the curtain aside. I saw Zahra and another girl lying next to each other on the carpet, their trouser cuffs rolled down past their knees and their legs raised in the air. I was shocked. The maulawi held a thin stick raised above his head. His other hand was fondling the other girl's thigh. Maulawi Rashid startled when he saw me. He snatched his hand away. "What do you want, older sister? How dare you barge into God's house like this."

I looked at the maulawi, at the girls' naked legs, and at the other little girls, staring fearfully at me. "*Baba-jan* sent me to bring Zahra home," I said. "She is sick."

In Afghanistan, to be taken seriously, a woman should be a messenger for a man, especially an elder.

Maulawi Rashid looked at me, then at Zahra. He shrugged. "She came late." He then turned to Zahra. "Get up and go, child."

He measured my body with those unblinking reptile eyes of his, then placed a finger on his lips. I grabbed Zahra's hot hand and ran. Once outside, I felt sick. I knew Maulawi Rashid. I had a bad feeling about his hand on that girl's thigh. On our way home, Zahra was silent. Wiping her tears away with the corner of her shawl, she held her Qur'an tight against her chest and wept. I felt very sad. Twice, I stopped to hug her. She was burning with fever.

I knew I had to speak to *Agha*. I had been too ashamed to tell *Agha* what Maulawi Rashid had been doing in the river, but this was my little sister. I had to speak up. That wrinkled hand on that little girl's thigh . . .

Night had fallen. Darkness blanketed the walls of our courtyard while the stars glittered overhead in their millions. The world was silent. How wonderful to sit on the terrace, gazing at the luminous, star-veiled night instead of cowering in a dark basement beneath a sky lit with bullets. *Agha* was no longer fighting the Russians. Now, he was reading Russian literature.

Herat's 120 days of wind season had begun. A gentle breeze was blowing through the branches, filling our relieved hearts with peace. The soft sound of zephyr at night allowed us to sleep deeply, undisturbed. How different the soft *hoo hoo* of the wind was from the fearful *Whoosh! Whoosh!* of Russian rockets. The world was so tranquil that night, I didn't want to ruin the calm atmosphere in our home by talking about that hateful maulawi. I let *Agha* read his novel, *And Quiet Flows the Don*. "What's it about, *Agha*?"

"It's about the Russian wars."

"War again?" I said.

Agha winked at me. "There's also a love story in it."

That night, Herat was the most beautiful city in the world.

The next day Zahra was diagnosed with chicken pox. She was too sick to go to school. The fever had weakened her, so *Agha* forbade her to go to the mosque. I was relieved because I hadn't found the courage to speak with him about Maulawi Rashid.

Mushtaq was still going to the mosque. I asked him whether Maulawi Rashid hit the boys. "All the time," he said. "If we don't do our homework, he makes us sit in a row with our hands raised and he whips them with a tree branch."

I was so angry! Why did he make the girls lie on their backs, bare their legs, and raise them into the air when the boys only had to lift up their hands?

A week passed. *Nanah-jan* began nagging, waving her *tasbeh*. "Thank God, she has recovered and can continue her studies at the mosque."

Baba-jan agreed. "If Zahra is healthy, she should go."

The decision had been made. I was very upset; I had to find a way to tell *Agha* what I had seen Maulawi Rashid doing in the river.

That night, I sat down next to *Madar* and *Agha* and hesitantly raised the issue. "*Agha*, must Zahra go to the mosque?"

My father looked puzzled, "Homeira, your sister has recovered. Your *Nanah-jan* and *Baba-jan* want her to continue her religious studies."

Madar nodded. "She should go."

My father knew I had something to say; I had never sat down between them and involved myself in their decisions before. *Madar* looked at me. "What is it, child? What's troubling you?"

I told them everything that I'd seen in the mosque—about how Maulawi Rashid became very nervous that I had seen his hand on a girl's thigh. I told them how he made the girls bare their legs for him to whip them, but the boys were only whipped on their hands. *Agha* listened carefully. When I'd finished, he kissed my forehead. "Go to bed, my daughter."

The next day when Zahra and I came home from school and ate lunch, Zahra picked up her Qur'an and put on her hijab. *Madar* stopped Zahra at the door and kissed her. "From now on, Zahra, *Baba-jan* will teach you the Qur'an."

A week later, I saw Maulawi Rashid performing his ablutions in the river. He pulled up his pants as soon as he saw me. I laughed in my heart. I had won.

When the school closed for the summer holidays, my family decided to visit Kababian village, always a happy excursion for us children after years of being pinned in by the war.

Baba-jan told Mushtaq to go tell Maulawi Rashid we'd be away on a vacation.

Mushtaq hesitated. "Maulawi *Sahib* doesn't allow kids to take a vacation," he said. "He'll think it's just an excuse, so I can avoid studying the Qur'an and play soccer instead. He might think that I don't want to pay his weekly stipend."

"Give Mushtaq the *panj-shanbegui* for the maulawi, so he can go on vacation," *Baba-jan* said.

"You give him the money," *Agha* replied. "I don't have money to waste on that man."

Hearing *Agha*'s words made me want to dance.

"Even with this money, Maulawi Rashid won't believe me," Mushtaq said. "Homeira should come with me." I was older and the family knew that Maulawi Rashid wouldn't bother me. He was eyeing his little students. Besides, Mushtaq was with me as an extra precaution. Even then, I don't know why I decided to go with him.

The streets were empty. When we reached the mosque gate, we paused at the entrance. Mushtaq handed me the money. "Homeira, you go inside. I'll wait here."

"Come inside with me," I said. I really didn't want to go into the mosque and face Maulawi Rashid alone. "You ask for your holiday and I'll confirm we're going away."

But Mushtaq pushed me through the gate. "Go! The *gaadis*, chariots, will be here any minute. I'll wait here for them."

There were two pairs of shoes in the courtyard beside the door to the mosque, a small boy's shoes and a pair of big shoes that I assumed were Maulawi Rashid's. Taking off my shoes, I quietly entered. I walked into the prayer hall. The mosque was empty. I clutched the money tightly in my hand. I parted the curtain and entered the girls' section. There was no one there either, but somebody had left a cup of green tea and a jar filled with *deshlamah*. Leaning down, I touched the teacup. It was still warm. Maulawi Rashid must be somewhere nearby. He wouldn't go outside the mosque barefoot. I had a bad feeling about the silence and emptiness of that place. The money was damp in my hand.

Then, in that heavy silence, I began to hear a low, muffled voice. I stopped, trying to determine where the sound was coming from. It was Maulawi Rashid's voice, hoarse, almost a whisper. I couldn't understand what he was saying. The sound of breathing: *Ahhh . . . ahhh.* No. *Someone* was saying *something*, very softly. I decided to find him.

Nanah-jan materialized before my eyes. "Leave Maulawi Rashid alone . . ."

I pressed my lips together. I didn't *want* to leave him alone. He hadn't left me alone that day by the river. And since that day, the image of him rubbing himself had haunted my nightmares. He hadn't left me alone at all.

The noise was coming from behind the *minbar*, the pulpit from where the maulawi ascends to preach the Friday sermon. The *minbar* was a wide set of stairs, enclosed on two sides, with a platform and railing at the top. The closer I got to the *minbar*, the clearer the sounds became. They seemed to be emanating from *beneath* the pulpit itself. I had never been behind the *minbar* before. The side of the *minbar* was open, enclosing the space beneath the raised platform, with a small door allowing entry that was half open. The voice was definitely coming from under the *minbar*, I could hear it clearly now, a small whimpering voice, *Take your hands off . . . take your hands off . . .* And ugly moaning sounds, *Ahhh . . . ahhh.*

I opened the gate. What I saw froze my hand to the door's wooden crossbar. Maulawi Rashid was sitting on the floor of the *minbar* with a six-year-old boy, whom I'll call Moneer, on

45

his lap. I'd seen Moneer in our street. Mushtaq said that he was a timid boy who didn't play with the other kids, sitting on the sidelines during soccer games.

Moneer's pants were down. His face was white with fear. When he saw me, he began to cry. Startled, the maulawi heaved the poor boy off his lap. Maulawi Rashid turned to me, shouting, "What are you doing here, shameless girl!"

I was speechless. The maulawi's turban was askew. His face glistened with sweat. Moneer stood completely still, tears trickling down his cheeks. Maulawi Rashid was shaking, unsure whether to pull up his own pants first or Moneer's. He hoisted his trousers up, then pulled up Moneer's. Maulawi stepped toward me, his face contorted with anger. I heard the *slap slap slap* of Moneer's bare feet as he ran away through the empty mosque.

Maulawi Rashid grabbed my arm, pulling me into the *minbar*. He thrust his face up against my own. "You open your mouth, little beauty, and I will bring you in here and . . ."

Moneer was gone. I was alone. It was me, Maulawi Rashid, and the *minbar*. The maulawi's breath stank like rotting meat. The stench of his sweat was overpowering. He tried to push me against the wall of the *minbar*. I wrenched my arm away.

"Homeira!"

It was Mushtaq. Thank God! Wild-eyed, Maulawi Rashid turned. Seeing my brother, he began shouting, spittle flying from his lips, "How dare you bring a girl with breasts into my mosque! You . . . !"

Maulawi Rashid turned back to me, his finger to his lips.

"Hush."

Mushtaq turned and ran. I backed out of the *minbar*, then walked quickly out of the prayer hall, keeping an eye on Maulawi Rashid. He was standing paralyzed at the door of the *minbar*. I was drenched in sweat, but the air felt as cold as winter. Maulawi Rashid's disgusting odor clung to me like a shroud.

Mushtaq was waiting at the mosque gate, his face ashen. We ran home. *Madar*, *Nanah-jan*, and *Baba-jan* were still waiting in the courtyard for the *gaadis*. Mushtaq sat down on the ground, trying to catch his breath. I sat down beside him, holding my head in my hands. The money slipped from my sweaty palm, landing in the dirt by my feet.

"Homeira! Why do you still have the money I gave you?" *Baba-jan* asked.

I opened my mouth to reply. Suddenly, I began to cry.

Madar hugged me. "What's wrong, Homeira? What's happened?

My little brothers and sister stared at me, silent and worried. I heard the sound of the horse-drawn carriages approaching from down the street, *clop clop clop. Sherang! Sherang! Nanah-jan* was watching me.

Agha came into the courtyard. "The *gaadis* are outside. Let's go." He looked at me, then at the worried faces of *Madar* and *Nanah-jan*. "Homeira, are you all right?"

"She went to the mosque to pay for Mushtaq's vacation," *Madar* said.

Agha's face went white. "Homeira! What happened to you at the mosque?"

Crying and sobbing, I told them everything. Tears welling in his eyes, my father hit his face again and again. *Baba-jan* kept repeating, *In the name of God! In the name of God!* while my *Nanah-jan* chanted, *God forbid!* over and over.

His face clouded with anger, *Agha* headed for the door.

Baba-jan intercepted him. "Wait! This is the entire neighborhood's problem, not just yours and mine. We must postpone the trip to the village and deal with this matter at once."

My brothers began to cry. They had no idea what had happened. But Zahra knew. She didn't ask why our vacation had been canceled.

I couldn't erase the image of the maulawi placing his finger on his lips. It wouldn't leave my eyes. His voice whispered in my ears:

"*Hush.*"

His body odor was stuck in my nostrils. His hand still gripped my arm. The *minbar* still pressed against my back. *Nanah-jan* kept on repeating, *God forbid . . . God forbid!* I was so frightened. I wished I had left Maulawi Rashid alone.

Before noon, the neighborhood elders assembled in our house. My mother made tea for everyone. I was sitting under the mulberry tree in our courtyard, unable to move. *Nanah-jan* made me a drink of rose water with sugar cubes, but I couldn't drink.

Voices were raised inside the house, but I couldn't make out what was being said. *Agha* told me to stay in the courtyard until he called me. Mushtaq sat silently above me in the mulberry tree. *Agha* planned to call my brother to testify as well. He wanted us to tell the elders what we had seen in the mosque.

Mushtaq called down to me, "Homeira! I didn't see anything."

I looked up at him, "We are supposed to tell them whatever we saw. So you must say what you saw."

Around noon, *Agha* called my brother and me into the house. I sat down behind my father. My body began shaking again. As soon as I started talking, the *adhan* echoed across the neighborhood. *Nanah-jan* always told us to remain silent during the *adhan*. "It is the *adhan*. You must listen and not speak. It is a sin if you talk during the *adhan*."

It was Maulawi Rashid's voice. I would not remain silent while that vile voice was in my ears! Mushtaq and I related everything that we saw, everything that Maulawi Rashid did and said. I spoke first; then my brother. After we had finished, *Agha* told our neighbors about Zahra's illness and what had happened to her at the mosque.

The elders sat silently listening, they didn't raise their heads to look at me or Mushtaq. Finally, one of them asked in a gentle voice, "Did you recognize that little boy? Do you know him?"

"Yes, it was Moneer," I said. Mushtaq nodded.

"Bring Moneer here," the man said.

Baba-jan held up his hand. "Please, it is better that we don't tell everyone about this. Moneer is young and he must grow up in this city. Think about his reputation. If you believe my two grandchildren are telling the truth, then the man we must confront is Maulawi Rashid."

Looking over at me, an old man with a long white beard said, "So, child, whatever you've said is exactly what you saw?"

I started crying. Wiping away my tears on my shawl, I said, "I swear on my *Agha*'s head that I am telling the truth."

That afternoon, I came down with a fever. By nightfall, it was much worse. During the night, *Madar* cooled me by placing wet towels on my forehead and my feet. I had a nightmare that Maulawi Rashid was crushing me in his embrace.

In the morning, I was too weak to get out of bed. Mushtaq came and whispered in my ear, "The men went and had a talk with Maulawi Rashid. You could hear him yelling from inside the mosque. He told them that you were sinful and a liar. Maulawi Rashid shouted, 'God will never forgive a false accusation.'"

The neighborhood elders gave Maulawi Rashid two days to leave the mosque. They began looking for another maulawi.

Two days later, Maulawi Rashid was gone. Moneer's name was kept secret by the white-bearded neighborhood elders. Mushtaq and I were warned not to say anything to anybody. Nodding his head, Mushtaq silently agreed. Because I was a girl, the elders were, ironically, less concerned about me gossiping. Now that my breasts had begun to show, I wouldn't be allowed to go out in the streets to see my friends anymore.

Dear son,

Today is your birthday. I no longer measure the annual cycle from the seasonal shift of spring and winter. Only when your birthday arrives do I feel another year has passed without you. I wait to hear about you, night and day. I wait, in the hope that someone will send me a picture of you. But I am in no hurry. I know full well that it may take a long time before we can see each other again.

I consistently missed the opportunities to see your "firsts" at this stage of your life. I only wish that I could have had the opportunity to hear your voice. Sometimes I am in such despair that I fear the pain will crush me. Still I am not thinking of giving up. I know that Islam has been turned into an instrument of retribution. It has been turned into a stone with which to strike people, especially women.

I have hired an attorney to petition the courts for the right to talk to you. The law must be stronger than the men of that land, I thought. But my attorney wrote to me last night, "The court has determined that the child belongs to the father under any and all circumstances." The court won't grant a mother her most basic rights.

My dear son, on your birthday I am as lonely a traveler as all the travelers in the world. A traveler who could not even for one last time wave at or kiss the face of the beloved she had left behind. A traveler with a big, empty, and heavy suitcase. I can tolerate the weight of most days away from you, but not the weight of being away from you on your birthday.

On your second birthday, when I was already gone, I sent you a doll and a few storybooks with colorful pictures. But your father had said, "What dead person can send gifts!" and never gave them to you. He would rather you think I am dead than longing for you. This is my punishment, I guess. So, on this, your birthday, I sit by a candle with this pen and paper near the window, wondering if I should have listened to Nanah-jan's warnings and respected the patriarchal order of the city. Then at least I would have you.

It's better I stop writing and pray that at the moment you blow your birthday candles, without your father noticing, you make a wish to God for my return to you. God can bring any dead person back to life.

Happy Birthday, my little one,
Happy Birthday, my lovely son,
Happy Birthday, my Siawash.

5

The Red Shoes

At the beginning of the civil war, our neighbor Sharifah, a good friend of *Madar*, had two children, a daughter, Ranaa, and Mohammad, their *Shah-Pesar*.

Ranaa was a few months older than I. She was born in the season when the pomegranates ripened, but I was born at the end of winter. Azizah always teased me that I was the offspring of a barren season. Mohammad was the same age as Mushtaq.

Sharifah had given birth to Mohammad at her mother's house in Zendahjan village. Sharifah's husband, Omar, a storekeeper, longed for sons. As long as I can remember in the years I was growing up, Sharifah was always pregnant. She used to visit us in her swollen burqa and sit groaning, in the throes of another pregnancy, while her daughters sat beside her in a row.

During the civil war, Ranaa and Mohammad often stayed with us. *Madar* was happy to keep her best friend's children safe from harm in our cellar. We used to play together under *Nanah-jan*'s watchful eyes. She had a strict rule that boys only played with boys and girls only with girls. Poor Mohammad was always crossing that red line. Whenever Ranaa, Azizah, and I were playing with dolls, Mohammad would sit down and begin to play with us. *Nanah-jan* would lead him by the hand back to where Mushtaq was playing marbles. Mohammad would pull Mushtaq's hair and scream until Mushtaq got mad, knocking him down and sitting on his stomach.

When I was nine, the warring factions declared a cease-fire during *Eid*, the post-Ramadan festival. *Nanah-jan* found some henna. She told Azizah to get Ranaa from her house so that we three girls could have our hands painted. I've always loved the smell of moist henna. Bolting out the door before Azizah, I ran through Sharifah's big wooden gate, calling, "Ranaa! Come! *Nanah-jan* has made henna for us!"

Sharifah appeared in the hallway, heavy with her latest pregnancy, with Mohammad following behind. She handed me a loaf of bread wrapped in a cloth. "Take this to your mother, Homeira-jan. It is all I have to offer. Mohammad and I will follow."

Azizah, Ranaa, and I waited and waited while *Madar* and Sharifah reminisced about past *Eid* feasts, long before I was born. "I remember the *sofrah* spread across the floor covered with cookies, *noqol*, raisins, roasted peas, and almonds," *Madar* said.

Azizah, Ranaa, and I sat in a row next to the henna bowl. Mohammad crawled over and sat down close to me. I tucked my skirt under my legs, so I wouldn't absorb the scent of a boy.

Placing small, triangular wrapping cloths beside her, *Nanah-jan* sat down in front of us. Mohammad was staring at the henna bowl. *Nanah-jan* took Azizah's hand in her own and began to draw henna patterns on her palm. *Nanah-jan* wrapped her *tasbeh* around Azizah's wrist and said, "Allah, for the sake of this day and night, keep war away from this land. Now, please, children, say '*Ameen*.'"

Everyone said "*Ameen*" in unison, except me. *Nanah-jan* hit my leg with the *tasbeh*. "Why are you silent, child? If you don't say '*Ameen*,' there will be no henna for you, Homeira."

"I will say '*Ameen*' to Mushtaq's jinni, *Nanah-jan*! Your *Allah* doesn't have a plate of rice for us, not even on *Eid*."

"You are such a silly girl! *Allah* doesn't concern Himself with such small things, child. If you don't say '*Ameen*' . . ."

I cried, "A bowl of rice is not a small thing."

Nanah-jan said, "You either say '*Ameen*' or your hand will never be decorated with henna."

"*AMEEN!*" I shouted. "*AMEEN! AMEEN! AMEEN!*"

I held out my hand. "*Nanah-jan*, please draw the jinni of the magic lamp on *this* hand and the monster Barzanghi on my other."

"What! Why would you want that, Homeira?"

I held my palms nearly touching. "I want the lamp jinni to fight with Barzanghi to see who wins."

Nanah-jan traced henna lines on my palm, then wrapped a cloth around my hand to hold the henna in place until it dried.

Next, *Nanah-jan* painted Ranaa's hands and wrapped them. There was a small amount of henna left in the bowl. Holding out his palm, Mohammad sidled over to *Nanah-jan*. "Please," he said, "paint a design on my hand."

We girls all laughed. "Mohammad smells like a girl!" I said, giggling. *Nanah-jan* used the rest of the henna to draw a star on

Azizah's hand, then tied a wrapping cloth around it. Mohammad crawled into his mother's arms and wept.

On the day of *Eid*, *Madar* gave bangle bracelets to Azizah,
Ranaa, and me. Mine were green, Ranaa's were red, and Azizah's
were yellow. We traded our bangles; every day I wore a different
color. Sharifah gave each of us two hard-boiled eggs without
names painted on them. Mohammad traded me his eggs for a
chance to wear my bracelets.

Arms outstretched, he began to dance in our yard. The
bangles tinkled like a tambourine as he swooped and twirled.
Sherang! Sherang! His face glowing, he asked if he could come
over and wear them again. I took pity on him because I'd so sel-
dom seen him smile. "Take them home with you. You can bring
them back tomorrow."

Mohammad's face clouded over. He smacked his lips. "I
can't. My father will kill me."

The next day, he brought a piece of *naan* for me, slid my
bangles onto his slender wrist, and danced again on our terrace.

"Your boy is spending all his time with the girls, Sharifah-
jan," *Nanah-jan* said when Sharifah came over to take her *Shah-
Pesar* home. "He must play with boys if he is to grow into full
manhood." Pregnant again and as large as a washtub, Sharifah
drew Mohammad to her, wiping her tears away with her shawl
as she slowly walked him home.

During the cease-fire, *Agha* brought me a pair of high-heeled
shoes. They were red and shiny with beads on their toes. When
I walked on the terrace, they talked to me with every step: *chek
chek chek.* I was very happy because they were too small for either Azizah or Ranaa.

One morning when the streets were drawing their uneasy breath in the lull before the crackle of gunfire, Ranaa knocked on our door, yelling, "Come quick! Hurry! The baby is coming!"

"Ranaa, you and Mohammad stay here," *Madar* said, throwing on her hijab. "*Baba-jan*, please look after the children. I'm going with *Nanah-jan* to help Sharifah."

"I hope it's a boy this time," Ranaa said. "My father will be so happy . . ."

"Your father isn't happy with Mohammad?" I asked.

Ignoring me, Ranaa began to play with one of my dolls.

Mohammad crawled over and sat next to me. He touched my hand. "Homeira, would you let me wear your shoes?"

"Which shoes?"

Mohammad looked at his feet. "The ones that make a *chek chek chek* sound when you walk."

"*Those shoes?*" I said, my mouth hanging open. "But they are red, they have beads on them . . . they are *girls' shoes!*"

"They are beautiful," he whispered and began to cry.

I begged Mohammad not to cause trouble for us. I was afraid that *Nanah-jan* would get angry if she heard I'd lent Mohammad my shoes, and Mushtaq was a terrible tattletale. I was afraid the ogre Barzanghi would come and drag me away to his lair.

Mushtaq brought over his marbles, but Mohammad pushed him away, tugging at my shawl and crying. Mushtaq disapprovingly ignored him and went over to a corner and began shooting marbles against the wall.

We girls lined up our dolls and had a tea party. Ranaa was the hostess and Azizah, I, and the dolls were her guests. She poured water in our glasses. "Have some nice hot tea, dears."

"Donkeys! Nobody serves tea without sweets," Mushtaq yelled from across the room.

"When people are dying of hunger because of the war, we should be grateful to at least have tea to drink," Ranaa replied.

Then, wrapping her shawl around her shoulders, just like *Nanah-jan*, she said, "Please, dears, enjoy your tea."

Suddenly, the stutter of machine guns shattered the silence. An angry swarm of invisible bullets buzzed outside the window. Woken from his nap, *Baba-jan* ran into the room. "Everyone into the cellar!" he shouted. He looked around. "Where's Mohammad?"

Mohammad was gone. The unseen bullets were everywhere. *Baba-jan* looked out the window. "My God!" he shouted.

He ran out into the courtyard. We children all gathered at the window. Mohammad was dancing in the yard wearing my red shoes.

Sharifah gave birth to another girl. Derisively telling Sharifah that her daughters were of no use to him, Omar left the house and didn't return for weeks. He said he was done with her. In the weeks that followed, *Madar* visited Sharifah often.

Omar's wish for posterity through a male lineage was never granted. Luckily, their house was never bombed and his brood of daughters all survived. After giving birth to eight girls, Sharifah's hair turned gray. "Every person's destiny is different," she told *Madar*. "Had I not given birth only to girls, I would be the luckiest woman in the world."

Mohammad and Mushtaq were no longer allowed to play with girls. We were grown up now and banned from the street. Mohammad spent most of his time sitting in his father's grocery store or going to the mosque with his father. I'd see him carrying water from the river to irrigate their fruit trees or sitting on the soccer field, watching the other boys play. He never joined a team or chased the ball around the field. I often saw him sitting on the riverbank, staring at the river.

"Our voices are now deeper than Mohammad's," Mushtaq said. "When he speaks, it is like a sparrow chirping. Whenever there's a scuffle with the boys from the next block, Mohammad runs away and hides behind a tree."

One day I was sitting under our mulberry tree reading. Suddenly, I heard yelling and the sound of running feet. In the distance, dogs were barking, their enraged howling getting louder by the moment. The shouting got closer. Mohammad and Mushtaq threw themselves into our yard, slamming the gate behind them. His chest heaving, Mohammad leaned against the wall, trying to catch his breath. I hadn't seen Mohammad in a while.

"Mushtaq, what happened?" I shouted. "Are you all right now?" I asked Mohammad.

He nodded. "I'm fine. Just keep the gate closed. Those dogs . . ." His voice was high and trembling.

Mushtaq was now taller and heavier than Mohammad, who had a delicate face with full lips and thin, arching eyebrows. "Look, Mohammad," I said. "Your feet are still the same size as mine." When I placed my foot next to his, I noticed a red stain on his white sneaker. "My God," I said. "You're bleeding!"

A trickle of blood was dripping onto the ground from the edge of Mohammad's shoe. Mushtaq's face went white. "Are you hurt?"

Mohammad wrapped his arms around his stomach. Mushtaq knelt down and rolled up Mohammed's trouser. A line of blood was running down his calf. Mohammad groaned, his face ashen. Mushtaq rolled the trouser cuff halfway up Mohammad's thigh, but the injury was somewhere higher. His leg was pale and shapely. And hairless. Mushtaq pulled his hands away as if they'd been scorched.

Mohammad bent over double and began to cry. Mushtaq reached for Mohammad's tunic. "Let me see your stomach. You must have cut yourself climbing over the wall."

Mohammad pushed Mushtaq away. The blood had darkened the crotch of his trousers. Mohammad's truth hit me like a clap of thunder on a cloudless day. All these years, that truth had been hidden beneath his clothes. Dumbstruck, I leaned against the wall. Mushtaq hadn't figured it out. I wrapped my arms around Mohammad. "Don't be frightened, dear," I said. "All us girls reach puberty one day. Yours is early and you didn't know."

Sobbing loudly, he leaned his head against my shoulder. Mushtaq screamed, his face frozen in shock.

Mohammad wiped his tears on his sleeve. "My mother told me to run home whenever this happens. This was all my father's idea. He made me wear boys' clothes, so our relatives would think that God had given them a boy. My father demanded a boy to remove the shame of a family of girls. My father threatened to divorce my mother and remarry if she didn't agree. He needed a boy to open the store and clean up before closing; a boy who could shop in the market."

Mohammad stepped out of my embrace and turned to Mushtaq. "My name is Afsanah. Only Ranaa, my mother, and father know."

Mushtaq was in shock. He wouldn't look at Afsanah. Suddenly, a high wall stood between him and his childhood companion; the door of their friendship had slammed shut.

Mushtaq and I kept Mohammad/Afsanah's secret safe for another two years. She hid behind Mushtaq whenever the boys were fighting. She cleaned her father's store, ran errands to the market, and prayed beside her father at the mosque. The neighbors all thanked God that Omar had at least one son to keep his household bathed in light. At night, when everyone was asleep, Mushtaq would sneak over next to me and talk about Mohammad/Afsanah, telling me about her laughter, her hair, her sparkling green eyes. He couldn't bring himself to call her Afsanah. For Mushtaq, she was Mohammad, a he.

Nanah-jan turned to Sharifah. "That son of yours, Mohammad, doesn't look or smell like a boy. You should pay more attention to him. Look at our Mushtaq! Hair is sprouting above his lips. His voice has grown deeper. He's turning into a man."

Mushtaq said. "*Nanah-jan*, what is the advantage of being a man? As soon as the back of our lips darkens we have to go to war."

The next day, Afsanah stopped by our house to borrow some yeast. I invited her in. We sat talking behind the window. "So,

Mohammad, when will you get a mustache?" I asked, winking. She laughed. "I can't wait to begin wearing girls' clothes, so we can spend more time together."

"*Insha-Allah*," I said, hugging her.

Nanah-jan began screaming. "What is it?" I shouted, jumping down from the window bench. "A rocket attack?"

"Homeira! How many years have I been telling you that boys play with boys and girls play with girls?" *Nanah-jan* yelled, swinging her *tasbeh* at me like a whip. "Have you no shame, girl, crawling into a boy's arms, where your breasts could touch his body!"

I ducked and ran to *Madar* while Afsanah ran out the door. "*Nanah-jan* is right, Homeira. You are fourteen now," *Madar* said. "Don't bring scandal down on our heads."

Nanah-jan began praying for me. "How could you do this to us? You smell like a boy now, God forbid! I wish I were blind so I'd never seen such wicked behavior."

Finally, baggy shirts and coats could no longer hide Afsanah's breasts. Overnight, she began wearing girls' clothes, was banned from the street, and the light was extinguished in Omar and Sharifah's household. Afsanah came over to visit wearing a black skirt and a red short-sleeved blouse, her breasts showing proudly beneath the fabric. Her hair now touched her shoulders. Mushtaq was in the yard when Afsanah removed her burqa. My brother's face lit up in a huge smile. Afsanah dropped her head and turned away, blushing.

All that afternoon, *Nanah-jan* drank glass after glass of rose water while Mushtaq and I laughed and laughed.

But the time of our joyous laughter didn't last very long. The civil war had spread throughout the country. The roads were barricaded by battling factions. Travel outside the city was extremely dangerous.

The warring factions entered Kabul and took over the government. The mujahideen groups who had stood together in protecting the people against the Russian invaders had now realigned along ethnic and tribal lines. Pashtuns, Tajiks, Uzbeks, and Hazaras splintered into hostile political factions, fighting each other for political control of the country. This internal power struggle was worse than the battles against the Soviet occupiers.

Herat was in ruins. Tens of thousands of people had died. Young people, the generation born in the 1970s and '80s, had been decimated, either killed in the wars or turned into refugees living in squalid tents beyond Afghanistan's borders. The face of my lovely city had been stripped of its beauty; only a jumbled skeleton remained.

Dear Siawash,

My heart was in knots this afternoon and I was filled with anxiety. I had a feeling that something bad was going to happen. Very early in the morning, I called Madar *at home in Herat. I knew she must've woken up for the prayer.* Madar *never goes back to bed after her morning prayers. She had the habit of starting her cleaning in the early hours of the dark of morning. After a few rings, I heard her calming voice and asked her if everything was all right. She took a deep sigh and said: "This land trembles in our hands and hearts every day, but nothing out of the ordinary has happened." In the background, I could hear the sound of running water and rattling dishes being washed.*

I couldn't help myself. It was as if there were fire under my feet. I called your Uncle Jaber. He didn't pick up the phone. I left a Facebook message for him. I asked him how things were in Kabul. His messenger light turned green. He responded at six in the morning and said, "When will you learn to live a life in your own time zone? It's six in the morning in Kabul. What could've happened?"

Jaber used to be rather short-fused. He was among those who blamed me for not being able to comply with society's demands. He wasn't rejecting me, but he always believed that what people say matters. He would say, "A woman is a woman, and it isn't right for a woman to get ahead of society's norms." Still, after your father didn't let me hear your voice or have a picture of you, Jaber felt sorry for me and said, "Being a woman is like being in quicksand. The more you struggle to stay afloat, the deeper you sink." But sometimes, Jaber seems to have turned into another Nanah-jan. He would say, "If you had accepted your womanhood, you wouldn't be suffering this much."

I told him that I had a sense that something was wrong, that you, Siawash, were sick or unhappy.

Jaber's reply: "Leave his son alone."

It's not just your uncle who does that: they all describe you as "his" son. Do you know how painful it is to hear that even my own family members consider you "his" son and not mine? Do they mean to hurt me, or are they just victims of the law and the patriarchal traditions? I have repeatedly objected and reminded them that you are my son as well, but my voice must sound weaker than the voice of the law and the traditions. How much can I fight with them?

But none of that matters as much as the reason I was speaking to him in the first place.

I had heard that there had been a suicide bombing across the street from where I think you go to kindergarten. A Facebook posting said that all the kindergarten windows had been shattered. You must have been very, very frightened.

So I was frantically trying to find someone who could tell me you were all right. All morning, I'd been scanning the images of the casualties on Facebook, looking for your face, hoping I wouldn't see you in the wreckage. Nobody had any news of you—dead or alive. But I'm not even sure I would recognize a picture of you.

I remember days when we were frightened, as you must have been. We lived in constant fear, scattering suddenly, like a flock of frightened birds. But at least in those days, I had Nanah-jan or Madar who would tell me stories to distract me from tasting the bitterness of war.

My son, I worry that if the Taliban have taken a position outside your kindergarten, and I am not there for you, who will be telling you stories to distract you?

6

Dancing in the Mosque

During the civil war, when I was searching in the silting waters of those ruined houses for the last of the living fish, *Agha* became addicted to the BBC. Hour after hour, he listened to the reports of the death tolls as the warring sides tore apart the fabric of our society. *Baba-jan* hung on every word of the news as well. Lying down in the heat of the day, he placed his old wooden radio on his stomach, always searching for a better frequency and clearer voice. But soon he would get frustrated hearing nothing but the horrible news of war; he would finally get up, cursing the radio as a wooden box filled with lies.

Madar showed no interest in the BBC. She said that the war and the killings reported by the BBC were disasters we experienced firsthand. What was the point in struggling with the war itself the whole day and then listening to it again at night? *Madar* believed the BBC only reported on the deaths of Afghan men. She said the station would never investigate the number of women whose lives were taken inside their own homes by stray bullets or bombs. And it was in November 1994, when I was just a teenager, that the BBC first introduced me to the word "Taliban."

That night I thought that the Taliban must be soldiers with high boots like the Russians, or with wide-bottom pants like the youth of the communist *Khalq* and *Parcham* factions, or maybe they are like the mujahideen. But the Taliban were like none of them. They were young men with beards and long hair and kohl eyeliner. They were tall and thin as if they had been starved for years. They didn't have boots but walked in ripped and torn sandals and slip-on shoes as if they had walked the entire distance from Kandahar to Herat on foot.

I had heard their name first on the BBC, but this was the first time I saw them. I saw them through the cracks from behind the front door when they were blaring their warnings that photos, televisions, or books from the lands of the infidels should not be kept in our houses. Soon I realized that they were very different from all the other fighters we had seen. They were not only dusty and depressing looking but ruthless and angry, too.

It wasn't long before the Taliban implemented sharia law in Kandahar. They closed all the girls' schools. Women and girls were forbidden to leave their houses. The Taliban ordered that no woman's face or form should be seen anywhere in public. Burqas became mandatory, and a woman who had a good reason to be on the street had to be accompanied by a *mahram*. Slightest infractions subjected women to public whipping with cables. Women accused of adultery were to be stoned or shot.

I listened to the radio and thought to myself, *Kandahar is very far from here. The Taliban will never set foot in Herat.* I pitied the girls of Kandahar, whose hopes for education vanished. I was so removed that I even wished for Kandahar to be in a different country.

Every day, on my way to school, I would recite *Al-Fâteha*, the opening chapter of the Qur'an, three times, praying that God would mislead the Taliban so they would never find their way to our city.

But one September morning in 1995, as I was ironing my white hijab, preparing to leave for school, everything changed. *Agha* had gone out to buy fresh-baked bread for our breakfast. He returned without any bread, pale and frightened. He leaned his bicycle against the tree in our courtyard and called out, *Ansari! Ansari!*

I watched *Agha* as he ran from room to room, searching for *Madar*. She appeared in front of us, broom in hand. *Agha* said, "Amir Ismail Khan, the governor, fled Herat last night. The Taliban have taken over the entire city."

Madar turned pale and leaned against the wall as if her legs would not support her. Mushtaq jumped up and down. "See, Homeira, your prayers were not answered! No rain will fall when a black cat prays. God never answers the prayers of girls."

I burned my hand on the charcoal-heated iron I was using to press the laundry.

My sister, Zahra, who was then in second grade, hugged me and cried while *Madar* held us in her arms, weeping silently.

Mushtaq looked at me, perplexed. "Why are you crying? I wish the boys' school were closed. *I* am the unlucky one. I wish I were a girl."

The Herat-Kandahar highway had fallen, one checkpoint at a time, like beads dropping from a broken necklace. Those white flags now fluttered above our city.

Almost immediately, you could feel the change. Suddenly, the streets were barren of women. Only men were allowed in the bazaars and markets. Female doctors were dismissed from the hospitals and sent home, except for a few in the maternity wards. Most women chose to have their babies at home because of the danger of being out on the street, even with a *mahram*. The Taliban beat women on the street on any pretext. In our neighborhood, a baby or a mother died in delivery almost every month.

During all those days, I was like a bird in a cage, my wings fluttering against the bars, still trying to escape. Herat's only functioning radio station was controlled by the Taliban, which broadcast nothing but religious chanting and Qur'anic recitations. So every night I listened to the BBC, expecting the radio to announce news of the Taliban's departure and the reopening of the girls' schools. I wouldn't go to bed until the newscast ended. Then, under my blanket, I would cry myself to sleep.

Madar said that Herat was full of lost sparrows. Sitting in the mulberry trees in our courtyard, I watched these tiny birds flitting from branch to branch. When they flew off into the blue sky, I wished that I could fly away with them. Once, I told Mushtaq that I wished I were a sparrow, too. He was kicking his soccer ball against the courtyard wall and catching it in his hand. He paused and thought for a second. "*Madar*'s burqa is large enough that you can put it on, grab the hem, flap your arms like a bird, and fly away."

I grabbed the soccer ball and hit him with it. He shouted and started chasing me. *Madar* stepped between us. "You should never fight with boys."

I sat on the terrace and cried my eyes out. "The Taliban are in Herat to stay. There is no likelihood of them leaving the city. There is no hope for the girls of Herat."

While gathering clothes from the clothesline in the courtyard, *Madar* said, "If anything could have been built from tears, I would have built an entire city. Instead of crying, Homeira, why don't you get up and do something?"

"*Madar!* What can *I* do? Shall I go out and fight the Taliban?"

"No! Taliban or no Taliban, it makes no difference. We cannot fight these men. You must fight against your attitude."

"What about you? I hear you weeping every night."

"Because I didn't learn to fight my attitude, to fight my despair." *Madar* looked at me, reminding me of my responsibility. "Do you want to inherit only tears and weeping from me? You can do better than that, Homeira."

The very next day, as *Madar* was sweeping the courtyard, she suggested that I turn our kitchen into a classroom. "This will help you pass your days more easily and it will also benefit our neighborhood girls. Without our help, they will grow up illiterate. Many of them have already passed their eighth birthday. They should have entered school last year. Every girl should learn at least how to write her name."

I said, "I have never been a teacher."

Smiling, *Madar* ran her fingers through my hair. "You are not a teacher; you are just the girl from the neighborhood. But you can become a teacher."

When *Agha* heard about our plan, he said that we must be very careful because it was very dangerous to defy the Taliban. *Baba-jan* was totally against the idea. He paced around the courtyard with his cane. "If the Taliban find out, it will be bad for the entire neighborhood and especially for Homeira. They will lash her mercilessly. Is that what you want? To see your daughter whipped in public? Believe me, if the Taliban see ten girls leaving this house, they won't stand by quietly and do nothing." He waved his cane in the air. "We survived the Russians. We survived the civil war. I won't allow us to be dishonored by Taliban whips."

Madar explained that by homeschooling the neighborhood girls I would be able to lessen the burden of loneliness. I would be able to stay in touch with friends. Besides, girls should not grow up illiterate. I thought to myself that if the girls remain illiterate, the Taliban would have accomplished their wicked objectives.

I was excited, even though I was afraid. I took my grandfather's hand in my own. "I really want to do this, *Baba-jan*."

For the next week, *Agha* thought and schemed, trying to come up with a safe way to create a school in our home. I said we should gather the neighborhood girls on the pretense of teaching them the Qur'an. *Baba-jan* protested. "Anything can be mocked, but one cannot mock the name of God and the Qur'an."

"*Baba-jan!* You can teach them Qur'an after I teach them reading and writing."

Baba-jan scratched his beard. Finally, he pointed his finger at me. "You speak to me as if I am opposed to educating girls. I am not. I am being pragmatic." Then he softened a bit. "We have to be very careful or these people will kill us." Then he picked up his cane and left for the mosque. "May God help us."

News of the homeschool spread rapidly among the girls. Mushtaq warned me, "I will not have *my* house filled with girls. If you do this thing, I will turn you in to the Taliban myself. I will blow your school up with a rocket-propelled grenade!"

I picked up a broom and chased after him. He ran out into the street. "I dare you to chase me!" he yelled, taunting me from across the dusty road. I could hear his laughter. I stopped in the shadow of our doorway.

I was thirteen the day I began homeschooling the girls. Our yard was so crowded with eager students that *Madar* moved her kitchen to a smaller room so that I could use the biggest room in the house for teaching. *Agha* borrowed a blackboard from the boys' school, where he was teaching.

Every now and then, Mushtaq would climb over the wall into the courtyard, shouting, *The Taliban are here! The Taliban are here!* The terrified girls would hide their notebooks in their Qur'ans and fall trembling into one another's arms. And my little brother would laugh and laugh and laugh. Even though we became used to his terrible and not very funny joke, we still shivered every time. Such naughtiness was expected of boys to tease and scare girls.

Over time, the girls grew up before our eyes; the corners of their shawls kept rising higher from the ground as they grew taller. *Madar* guarded the classroom with a watchful eye, winter and summer, stitching colorful birds that would never fly away. While I learned to be a teacher, she sat patiently every day drawing flowers on cloth panels and embroidering them, stitch by stitch. She believed that one day, all those colorful birds would flap their wings and fly away, out of the stitches of the woven cloth into the clear blue sky.

The Taliban forbid any painting or needlework that portrayed people or any other living things. They claimed that drawing the images of living beings was a terrible sin. As she sewed, *Madar* would nod her head and say, "My life was full of obstacles."

Many nights, I dreamed that the sky was darkened with flocks of birds. They were coming in the thousands, flying into our courtyard, filling every room in our house. They picked up *Madar* in their beaks, lifting her into the air. I dreamed that shining stars were tangled in my mother's beautiful hair, falling to the earth like fiery sparks as the birds carried her away. I saw *Madar*, pinioned by a thousand beaks, growing smaller, then disappearing amid the cloud of birds.

Waking from my nightmare, I jumped up and ran to *Madar*, the vision of her beautiful star-filled hair lingering in my mind, only to find her tresses hidden beneath her scarf. I tenderly touched her sleeping face and returned to my bed.

Opium commands a very high price in the developed world. Before the arrival of the Taliban, however, opium was very cheap in Afghanistan. Farmers could barely survive regardless of what they planted. But when the Taliban came to power, they manipulated the price of opium by monopolizing its cultivation, harvesting, and trade. Their enormous earnings then allowed them to purchase weapons, pay their troops, and implement sharia law. Adding to the war suffering, a severe drought spread across Afghanistan, causing many crops to fail, and people from the countryside and small villages fled to the larger cities looking for work.

The drought laid to waste crops in the fields, and devastated the shrubs and trees, especially the apple orchards. One day I asked *Baba-jan* why God had punished the apple trees. It wasn't the fault of those trees that men had planted opium. My grandfather threw me a stern look. "If the wrath of God comes to a forest in the form of fire, it will burn *all* the trees, whether dead or alive."

Terrible suffering was inflicted on Afghanistan in those years. In addition to the poverty, drought, and despair, gossip, fear, and superstition rampaged through the streets like a pack of starving dogs. The women as well as the men bombarded us with countless fables and legends implying that all these miseries that befell us were the wrath of God.

The city of Herat was in the grip of a drought and economic collapse, but conditions were somewhat better than in the villages. Thousands of families from the surrounding region fled to Herat. The area across the small river in front of our house had been turned into an arid wasteland by years of Soviet bombing and tank treads and the subsequent destruction of the civil war. Ruined houses and shattered plots of land, once home to dozens of families, stood empty and abandoned. Little by little, this desolate landscape became filled with a legion of tents, each housing a family displaced by drought, famine, and war.

The few international NGOs that dared to remain in Afghanistan had provided the displaced families with tents for shelter. Eventually, the neighborhood mosque became too small to accommodate the male refugee congregants. So a large old tent was erected across the river from our home to serve as their mosque.

As time passed, more and more people from Ghor Province settled across the river from our house. We called them the "tent people." Our neighbors began to greet the refugees with smiles and kind words.

In those days, I lived the life of a bat. I could only appear at night, once darkness fell and when the city's heart stopped beating. I would open the front door wide and try to discern the river through the blackness, the vague shadows of walls along our street, and the jagged field of black tents pitched in the rubble, lit only by frail lantern flames winking in the night. I knew there were so many children in those tents, who, just like me, loathed boiled potatoes and cried for a simple plate of rice.

In the dark of night, I would hear the call for prayer. There was no other music on the streets, it was forbidden, just these *adhan*, chanted five times a day. In this utter silence, in this utter darkness, the city had become a ghost town.

Sometimes, in that silent darkness, the crying of a baby reached me from the tents, a sorrowful sound that wounded my heart. But the most plaintive sound in that ghost town was the somber but beautiful voice of a mother singing lullabies. These sweet, sincere melodies rose from among the tents, and sometimes from the high-walled houses beyond. Clear, sad notes that floated on the air and took back the night from the muezzin.

Several months after the arrival of the tent people, *Agha* told us he had noticed the youngest refugee girls gathering across from our house before and after classes. I told *Agha* that I had seen them as well, standing next to each other on the riverbank, staring at our house. I assumed that they also wanted to learn to read and write.

The girls from the tents had befriended the girls in my classroom. They knew exactly what was going on in our house. One day three of the refugee girls knocked on our door and begged me to allow them in the classroom. They swore they would tell no one, not even their own families. I told them that we had so many girls from the neighborhood, there was no more space in the classroom. The girls left our home with tears in their eyes, dragging away a piece of my heart.

I said we should find a way to teach in the mosque tent. I asked *Agha* to meet with the refugee parents to see if they would agree to let me teach their girls. They also absolutely had to agree to keep our school a secret.

After discussions with *Agha*, the tent people agreed to allow us to use the mosque tent for teaching their girls, but only if my lessons began after the noon prayer and ended before the late-afternoon prayer.

The tent people made *Agha* promise that in addition to reading and writing, I would teach their children the Qur'an.

I'll never forget the first day. *Agha* strapped the heavy

blackboard on his back. He took a circuitous route to the mosque to avoid a Taliban checkpoint located close to the encampment. With great anxiety, he crossed the Injil River bridge, entered the tent mosque, and leaned the blackboard against one of the tent poles. The refugee children began clapping and cheering. I placed a finger on my lips. "Have you forgotten your pledge already? What was our agreement? We are not to do *anything* that might upset the mullah."

After that day, it became *Agha*'s responsibility to fetch the blackboard from our home right after the noon prayers, circumvent the Taliban checkpoint, cross the narrow bridge over the river, and carry it into the tent. At the end of our class in the mosque, before the late-afternoon prayer, *Agha* carried the board back to our house so that it would be ready for my morning class.

Soon, a number of refugee boys joined my classroom in the mosque. They were very young and full of energy. Their presence breathed new life into our placid, fearful group of girls. The boys didn't want to attend school in the city. We asked their parents to keep their boys in the official school because of the added risk. But the boys rebelled. They complained that the teachers taught them nothing except Qur'anic recitation, Arabic, hadith, and sharia. "We are not allowed to play, the teachers hit us, and they force us to wear heavy turbans, even in the hottest weather."

Teaching a class of boys and girls together was another red line that I crossed.

Over the months, the children learned to speak softly. Even the rowdiest boys understood the danger and usually behaved.

We were like mice, silent and nervous, hiding in the walls from a hungry cat that could pounce on us at any time.

I had been teaching for nearly nine months in that huge tent made of heavy canvas. Thin shafts of sunlight entered through a few scattered holes in the tent's worn fabric, casting dust-filled beams of light into the shadows. The floor was trampled earth, with a few threadbare carpets to soften the rocks and pebbles. Not a breath of wind moved within the canvas walls.

It was so hot that one could smell the melting plastic from the children's cheap footwear.

The mullah had warned the children time and again not to leave their shoes inside the mosque. But because their shoes were cheaply made in Pakistan from recycled plastic, and because they were the only shoes they owned, and because these shoes would melt into colored puddles of plastic if left outside under the blazing sun, the children chose to defy the mullahs. I had suggested that the children hide their shoes beneath a fold of the tent where it touched the earth, but they wouldn't listen to me.

The afternoon was the worst time to enter the mosque. The foul smell of perspiring bodies and unwashed socks was overwhelming. The stench made breathing difficult and became even worse as the afternoon grew hotter.

The children begged me to roll up two of the mosque's canvas walls to allow at least some of the stinking air to escape. But I didn't dare because of the Taliban checkpoint.

The other advantage of keeping the tent flaps down was that

they served as curtains, so I didn't have to endure the ordeal of my burqa. The pleats of the fabric hindered my movements, wrapping around my feet. I often stumbled when walking and sometimes fell. My vision was limited to a small rectangular mesh in front of my eyes. It was difficult enough to see the children in the dim shadows within the mosque, but it would've been almost impossible when wearing my burqa.

On days when I had to hide within my burqa, my brain became so badly stewed that I often forgot to check my students' homework and exercise books. Sometimes I even forgot their names. But even on the hottest days, I never forgot when it was time to chase the children from the tent and slip away myself.

I was teaching during *Cheleh Tamuz*, the hottest month of Herat's 120-day season of heat, humidity, and wind—a dusty time of burning sun and torrid temperatures. Each day, one or two students suffered nosebleeds during class. The girls flapped their shawls to cool off while the boys fanned themselves with their notebooks, hidden within the pages of their Qur'ans.

It was during one of those steamy summer days—the time of year when the mulberries ripen on the banks of the Injil River and fall into the water—that we dared to dance in the mosque.

On that hot, dusty, fateful day, the girls were sitting in a circle telling stories while the boys listened quietly. The students jumped up and greeted me in unison in their high-pitched voices, "*Salaam, Moalem Sahib*. Greetings, madam teacher."

"Greetings to you, my students." I looked to my right and left to make certain that the mosque's entrance and exit curtains were rolled all the way down.

The girls fanned themselves with their shawls and said,

"Madam teacher, it is so hot in here. The mosque has turned into hell."

I loosened my shawl from my neck and looked around. "Why are there so few of you here today? Where are the other girls and boys? Does anyone know?" I asked.

Yarghal jumped up, laughing. "Madam teacher, last night we had a wedding here in the tent city. Shah Mohammad Khan's daughter married Ghafoor Khan's son." Yarghal waved his arm with his hand bent over. "Shah Mohammad Khan's daughter has one hand shorter than the other, like so!"

The boys all laughed. Then Faisal shouted, "No! You're wrong, Yarghal. Her one foot is shorter than the other." He stretched out his legs and twisted his hips so one foot appeared shorter. "Like this!"

Zarghuna, another student, stood up, holding her hands together in front of her shawl. She glanced down at Yarghal and Faisal, then looked me in the eye. "Madam teacher, it is a lie." She continued, "The eyes of the boys are all crooked." She turned to the boys and crossed her eyes, "Like this!"

The girls covered their faces with their shawls, their laughter fluttering around the darkened mosque like the chirping of sparrows. I couldn't help but laugh as well. I turned to the boys. "It is not honorable to make fun of a woman's appearance," I said. "*Especially* if it is not true."

The boys groaned. "*Moalem Sahib*," Yarghal said, "you *always* side with the girls."

"Of course," I said. "I *am* a girl. We must look out for each other. Now, tell me, why is the class so much smaller today?"

Yarghal stood up again. He held on to the waist of his

oversize pants with one hand while he gestured with the other. "Last night there was a wedding celebration. And today was the *takht-jamee* party, the post-wedding ritual welcoming the bride to her new house, so the girls went there to dance."

Under the Taliban, dancing was strictly forbidden. Shah Mohammad Khan had commandeered an abandoned house with high walls and an inner courtyard. The wedding guests arrived furtively, a few at a time, and made their way inside, while the groom's brothers, armed and vigilant, kept watch. Perhaps Shah Mohammad Khan had bribed the Taliban to stay away. And they must have played the wedding music very softly. Weddings among the refugees were usually quiet, somber, and joyless affairs, but Heratis still found ways to celebrate marriages in private.

Faisal raised his hand. "Most of the girls have not come to learn today, but we boys are all here. Those silly girls know nothing but dancing. As soon as they hear the sound of the tambourine they start twirling their shawls and waving their arms, and . . . and start"—Faisal made a face as if he had just eaten a bitter lemon—"dancing."

Bilal raised his hand. "No, teacher, some of the boys have also not come to the mosque today. They also went to the groom's house to watch the girls dance."

"Zarghuna danced very nicely last night at the wedding," Mahrukh whispered. "She is a very good dancer. All the women clapped for her."

"Is she telling the truth?" Yarghal asked. "You, Zarghuna, with the crooked hands and the crossed eyes know how to dance?"

"Is this really true, Zarghuna?" I asked. Although it was really no surprise. At eleven, Zarghuna was one of the most graceful girls in the class, with delicate hands and arms that moved like the wings of a swan when she adjusted her shawl. I could imagine her twirling to the jingling of the tambourines. She was a beautiful child; it pained me to think about what her future held.

Zarghuna blushed again, lowering her eyes. "Mahrukh also danced," she said, very softly.

I turned to the two girls. "I did not know that you even *knew* how to dance. Well done, my girls!"

Zarghuna's blue eyes glowed and Mahrukh's rosy face blossomed into a smile. I glimpsed Monisah nodding her head. A shy, tiny creature with dark skin, she was sitting, as usual, beside the blackboard with her shawl wrapped around her face. She drew her shawl away from her mouth.

"Wait!" I said. "Monisah wishes to tell us something. You may speak, my dear."

Monisah looked down at the dirt floor. "Can you also dance, madam teacher?"

"What a donkey!" Yarghal said. "When someone becomes a *moalem*, they must know *everything*."

The boys all started laughing. I tried not to laugh. I didn't want to hurt Monisah's feelings. "Hush! Hush! Students, you *must* be quiet. Please! Children! We must not make so much noise."

I smoothed my shawl with my hands. "I am not a dance teacher. I am your reading and writing teacher."

Zarghuna said, "Dear teacher, it is a pity that you don't know how to dance."

Yarghal jumped up. "I've got it!" He pointed at Zarghuna. "You, Zarghuna, can teach our teacher how to dance." Then he pointed at me. "And you, *Moalem Sahib*, can teach us how to read and write."

The girls laughed. Zarghuna turned to me. "Do you accept, dear teacher?"

A hot breath of mischief stirred in my soul. "Yessss!" I said. "But on the condition that we begin today."

Everyone started laughing and clapping. Zarghuna said, "There is *one* condition. There can be no boys here."

"Where should we boys go on this hot afternoon?" Faisal asked. "This is hell, but it is the only shade."

"I am not moving!" Yarghal said.

I raised my hand again. The class went silent. "I will learn to dance on another day."

I turned to Zarghuna. "Would you perform the dance that you danced last night?"

Mastorah said, "Madam teacher, the Taliban will come. They will hear us."

Faisal said, "We won't clap. We will watch quietly."

Mahrukh nudged Zarghuna's shoulder. "Stand up, dear, our teacher wants to see you dance."

Zarghuna shook her head and pointed toward the sitting boys. "Dear teacher, I am afraid that these boys will tell their families that I danced in front of them."

"We are not gossips!" Shahab said. "It is women who gossip."

Lailuma waved the corner of her shawl at Shahab. "You, Shahab, for shame! I see you every evening in front of the mosque gossiping with the others."

Yarghal said, "I am the worst gossip in the class and I swear that I will keep my mouth shut."

The other boys nodded.

I said, "I will stand by the tent wall to keep an eye on the Taliban checkpoint. It is the afternoon guards' shift. They are lazy in the heat and will be sleeping in the shade."

Monisah pulled her shawl away from her face. "I am frightened, teacher."

Zarghuna scowled at her. "I would dance in front of these boys, but *you* are afraid."

"Let me stand by the entrance curtain," Faisal said. "I have seen the mullah spying on us. One day, if I had not hidden my notebook inside my trousers, he would have found out we are not writing *aayas* from the Qur'an in our notebooks. I think he is suspicious of you, dear teacher."

"Is someone here gossiping about our classroom?" Zarghuna asked, searching the other children's faces.

"The mullah came to our tent and told my father not to have us children commit immoral acts in the mosque," Mastorah said. "And my father said, 'It is you elders who are immoral. These children know nothing about immorality.'

"Then the mullah warned my father that it is a mistake to have boys and girls mixed up together. He said the boys will learn evil habits from the girls."

There was a shocked silence.

"I think it is time now for Zarghuna to dance," I said. I positioned myself beside the mosque's entrance tarp, keeping a sharp ear for any footsteps outside. Zarghuna stood up and walked over to *mehrab*, a niche where the mullah usually stands to lead the prayers. She held the ends of her shawl in her hands and began to dance lightly on her tiptoes. Her arms floated on the air like a bird's wings, feathered by her many-hued shawl, while her fingers fluttered like leaves in the wind. Her midnight hair reached below her waist, swaying to the right and left in tempo with her supple movements. Her head turned from one shoulder to the other, following her dainty steps. Her shawl flew out around her as she spun, a luminous crimson cloud that floated on the heavy air. Her eyes were downcast in modesty and her cheeks were flushed to the color of roses. I had never noticed before just how beautiful she was.

I took a quick peek outside into the blinding afternoon light. The street in front of the tent was empty. Shading my eyes, I squinted into the distance. The checkpoint was also empty. I stepped back into the tent to watch Zarghuna. I began to clap in tempo to her movements. I could not stop myself; I was entranced.

And then the girls began to clap in time to Zarghuna's steps. The boys soon followed. The seated children were swaying back and forth as if listening to some unheard mysterious music. Yarghal's face was shining. "Do *you* know how to dance, Yarghal?" I said, raising my voice above the clapping.

Yarghal jumped up and began to dance around Zarghuna, his arms outstretched and his hands pirouetting at the wrists, mimicking her delicate movements. "Now we are sure that Yarghal will not gossip," Faisal said, laughing. "He's in the middle of this for everyone to see."

Yarghal glanced over at me. "Come on, dear teacher! It is *easy* to dance."

It was magical. The mosque was transformed. We were all laughing and clapping. The oppressive heat was forgotten. The notebooks were hidden in the Qur'ans and the girls hid their pens in their hair. Faisal drummed his hands on his knees. Zarghuna danced around the tent pole at the center of the mosque, her face radiant, while Yarghal circled around her, trying to imitate her steps. Shy Monisah's shawl had fallen away from her face. Her smile lit up the shadows.

"Well done, students!" I called. "Your dancing deserves a grade of one hundred percent."

Suddenly, I heard a noise beyond the fabric wall. I froze. I saw a stick lifting the heavy curtain that formed the door to the mosque. The muzzle of a rifle appeared, but the Talib's face was still hidden outside. I could only hope that he hadn't seen me in the dimness of the mosque. The curtain drew back farther. Now I could see heavy black boots and the black cuffs of baggy trousers. Our noise must have drawn the Talib's attention on his way to the checkpoint.

I flew to the center of the mosque, hoping the shadows would hide me. The children must have seen the fear on my face. They scattered like frightened pigeons before a stalking cat. Zarghuna collapsed onto the floor as if shot and threw her shawl over her head. The girls huddled together, hiding their faces behind their scarves. The boys scrambled to the back of the tent and sat down quickly in a ragged row. Poor Yarghal dove under the *minbar*. In the sudden, complete silence, I could hear the Talib's stick sliding along the thick fabric at the mosque's entrance.

I was trembling so much that I could barely lift up my burqa. My legs were about to collapse. Softly and very slowly I put the burqa over my head. I did not know whether it was better to confront the Talib at the entrance or wait where I stood until he entered the mosque. I doubt I could have taken the ten steps to reach the entrance anyway.

Then the Talib stepped inside. His voice rang out through the tent. My heart stopped. I was too frightened to understand what he was saying. He spoke again, his beard shaking with anger. He lifted up the thick canvas with his hand to let in more light, squinting into the shadows. He was a tall man, dressed in black, with a long, thin face set beneath a huge black turban. His hooded eyes, lined in black kohl, were like two drops of midnight. When he swiveled his head, searching the tent, his stare reminded me of a vulture, the bird that only feasts on the dead. His long black beard hung from hollow cheeks, almost hiding his narrow, bloodless lips. The muzzle of his Kalashnikov swung in an arc across the room, following his eyes.

He started shouting, but my ears were filled with the thumping of my heart. I tried to breathe slowly under my burqa. My hands were sweating. My knees were trembling. My head was spinning. The entire city was falling on my head. I didn't think I would be able to stand much longer; my whole body wanted to lie down and crawl away into a corner. The Talib barked again.

Then another Talib stepped into the tent from behind the canvas. He was younger and seemed much calmer. His face was pale, and his thin beard was almost blond. His rifle was slung on his shoulder. The older Talib was still shouting. The younger Talib made a gesture for silence. This surprised me. He leaned forward, squinting. "This mosque is as dark as a grave," he said. "What is going on here?"

Blackbeard stopped shouting and his beard stopped moving. The young Talib asked again, "What are you doing here? My comrade"—he pointed with his chin at Blackbeard—"told me he heard noises and clapping." His gaze swept the huddled children. "Is that true?"

I relaxed a little. They probably had not seen us dancing. I started to explain. Blackbeard shouted at me in Pashto. The young Talib raised a calming hand and said in Dari, "My comrade says you must not speak because we are not *mahram*, so it is sinful to hear your voice."

Blackbeard slapped his stick against the tent wall and spewed out more angry phrases in Pashto. The young Talib shrugged and turned to the boys. "Boys, tell me, *what is happening here?*"

The poor boys were shaking worse than I was. Before they could answer, I spoke again, hurrying my words so as not to be interrupted. "The boys are reading Qur'an, distinguished *sahibs*. See, they have their Qur'ans open. They were chanting the *surahs* and we were clapping to encourage them so that we may all better understand the words of Allah and His Prophet, peace be upon Him."

Blackbeard struck his stick on the ground, the noise echoing through the tent, like blows on flesh. His shaggy eyebrows frowned together like a thundercloud. I knew that it would anger him to hear the sound of my voice, but I was terrified of what the boys might tell him. Blackbeard spat more angry words into the deathly silent tent. The young Talib translated. "He said, some girl was standing and spinning around. What was *that*?"

Before anyone else could answer I said, "She recited her verses wrong and wouldn't sit still, so I made her spin around like a punishment to make her dizzy and tire her out."

In the commotion when the Taliban entered, Yarghal had crawled out from under the *minbar*, sneaking over to sit with the boys. Now, I saw he had his head between his knees with his hands clamped over his mouth to stifle his laughter. Seeing his shaking shoulders, I began to giggle within my burqa. Zarghuna hid in Mastorah's arms and they covered their heads with their shawls. They, too, were whimpering with laughter. The Taliban must have thought they were weeping with fear.

Blackbeard struck the ground again, then turned on his heel, muttering something in Pashto. He stalked out of the tent, hitting the entrance flap with his stick as he disappeared. The young Talib turned to me. "There should be no more clapping or laughing, understood?"

I stayed silent. I didn't dare say a word. The Talib turned and faced the children. "Do you understand me?" he said loudly, although I think there might have been a trace of a smile on his lips.

The children answered in unison, "*Yes, Sahib!*" The young Talib turned on his heel and left the mosque.

The curtain swung closed, eclipsing the fierce afternoon light, leaving the mosque in darkness and utter silence. I crept to the curtain and peeked out. The two Taliban were standing at the checkpoint, holding their rifles, looking in the other direction.

I stepped back into the tent and collapsed onto the ground. I removed my burqa slowly and looked around. I felt suddenly very old and very tired. The poor girls were huddled together, holding on to one another trembling. The boys were wide-eyed and as white as ghosts. Then Yarghal began to laugh. He rolled over onto his back and held his stomach, snorting with laughter. He pointed at me. "You were *so* afraid, *Moalem Sahib*, I thought you were going to faint."

All the boys began to laugh.

"*I* was afraid?" I said, relief flooding through my body. "*You* crawled under the *minbar*. I thought you would burrow into the earth like a hedgehog."

"How will you ever learn to dance now, teacher?" Faisal asked, chuckling.

"We girls will go to our teacher's house to provide instruction without you foolish boys," Zarghuna said, her voice ringing like a bell in the gloom.

I leaned back against the tent pole and gazed up at the canvas ceiling. It seemed so high that no one could ever reach it.

I looked over at the colorful pile of small shoes. Their neon colors glowed dimly in the shadows. I raised the curtain of the mosque to bring light into this dark place. Herat's warm winds covered us in the dust.

I believe that on that day in that sacred place, God smiled on us and loved us more than ever before.

My dear Siawash,

The first word you uttered was "Mothe." One morning, you had woken up in your white bed and you called me

"Mothe." My hands froze in place on the laptop keyboard as I was working on my latest book. It was your first resolute utterance, calling me "Mothe." I kneeled behind your bedroom door. Your voice had sent shock waves through me. Joy and excitement ran through every blood vessel in my body. I deliberately delayed entering your room so you could call me again, "Mothe." My spirit had been transformed because you were calling me by the most dignified word in any language . . . I came in, stood over your crib, and lifted you up in my arms. Spontaneously I held your hand in mine and I danced with you. You were puzzled by my excitement and were calling me "Mothe" again and again. It took you a whole month to complete your first word . . . "Mother."

Later I would stand in waiting behind your bedroom door so that I could hear you call me "Mother." I would place your little ball out of your reach, so you could call me "Mother." I would pick up my purse pretending to be leaving the house, so you could pleadingly call me "Mother." At night when your sleepy head would grace my chest, I would gently ruffle your hair, so your sleepy eyes would open and you would object with the word "Mother." In the mornings when you would open your eyes, I would close mine, pretending to be asleep, so you could attempt to wake me up, calling me "Mother." In the park of our housing complex, I would hold you back from the rides, so you would demandingly call me "Mother."

My son, it feels like eons since the last time you called me "Mother."

Today was Mother's Day in the United States. After work, I went to the best candy store I could find. I searched for the best chocolate I thought you would like, so when and if I am allowed to see you again, I will fill your mouth with sweets and you will call me "Mother"!

I've come to stroll on the beach. At night when the sands become cold, the oceanside becomes dark, my tears are allowed their privacy. On the beach, there's an occasional seagull, perhaps a lost flip-flop or maybe an apple with a bite mark. There, on the washed sand, a safe distance from the incoming waves, I write "Happy Mother's Day!"

From my earliest days, Madar *called me* osiyangar, *a rebel. I understand how frightening it must be for a mother to see her daughter break all the inviolable rules and customs of her repressive land. But, Siawash, I want you to be a rebel, to grow up to fight the antiquated, brutal ways of that land.*

My son, nothing can diminish this sense of motherhood in me. Let your uncle Jaber refer to you as "his son," but you and I both know the truth.

7

The Schoolgirls' Bathhouse Uprising

The popularity of needlework among Herati girls flourished during the Taliban house confinement of the women because it gave them something to do at home. But it is an art form that my sister and I never learned, in defiance of *Nanah-jan*'s wish to turn us into model brides. Years earlier, when *Madar* did not have permission to attend painting classes, she took up embroidery as an outlet for her creativity. But for me, needlework was an impediment to reaching important goals in my life.

Our life was compressed to stifling obscurity behind those curtained windows. Girls could only see the light when they parted the curtains to thread their needles. In such circumstances, there was only one place left for the women: the *hammam*, the public bathhouse. *Hammams* were safer than our homes, which the Taliban often raided, searching for televisions, radios, and even books.

It didn't take long for an idea to begin to germinate in my head. Maybe we could band together to study secretly.

I spoke with two of my classmates, who suggested I speak to the older girls, who crowded into a different corner of the bathhouse. I found my courage one day, and crawled between them on the tiled floor. "Hi," I said quietly.

They were talking about makeup and henna, a new color of nail polish, and whether to file their nails round or square. It made me sad that these same girls who last year were competing over half a grade difference on their exams were now gossiping about love marks and having babies.

One of my classmates asked me, "So, Homeira, you want to find a husband now because the schools are closed?"

I lowered my voice. "No! A husband is not the solution to our problem. We have to do something to return to our studies."

A few weeks later, one Wednesday around noon, I stood on my stool and said "hello" in a loud voice. They all turned and looked at me.

"I am Homeira," I said. "I am one of the girls from the lower grades."

For a second everyone was quiet. Then, one by one, they began to laugh.

"Well, dear," one of them began, "we are not in school anymore, we are in the *hammam*. Why are you talking like that?"

One of the girls held a plastic shampoo bottle close to my mouth like a microphone. "Here you go, Homeira-jan. Speak. We are all listening."

The girls began laughing hysterically. "Calm down, little

chick," someone shouted. "We can hear your peeping without the stool."

It took a few minutes for the older girls to realize that I wasn't going to sit down until they heard me out. Finally, they quieted down.

"Imagine the day that the Taliban finally leave," I continued. "The schools will be reopened, but the world will have passed you by as you will all be in your husbands' homes. Won't that be a shame? The world will say that Afghan girls were all waiting for the Taliban to come along so that they could get married and avoid an education."

I had planted a seed of rebellion in the girls in the bathhouse. Now we had to be patient and gather more allies to our cause.

The next time I returned to the bathhouse, everything was as usual. The girls were all sitting on their bathing stools, congregating. One of the upper-grade girls pointed at me. "Our chick commander wishes to address us."

I straightened my shoulders, placed my stool in the middle, and stood on it for a stump speech. The laughing got louder. I laughed with them and then waited for the clamor to subside. The chamber grew quiet with expectation. I thought to myself that I must be the only rebel who had ever given a public speech without a single stitch of clothing to a convocation of stark-naked girls.

"I am not a commander, but I do have a question: For how much longer are we willing to accept these tyrannical laws without a fight?"

"The Taliban make the laws, not you," somebody shouted.

"It's time we make our own laws," I said. I raised my voice.

"We should think about matters beyond the threads and needles we use for embroidery."

A voice called out, "Seriously, what can we do when all the men have fled the battlefield?"

I raised my hands for silence. "Good question. The past wars were between men, but now, the Taliban have declared war on women, so we are a party to this war and must fight for ourselves."

"I agree with the chick commander," a girl called out. "They have shut us up in our houses because they are afraid of us."

"You are wrong!" someone else shouted. "They think we are intellectually inferior to them. What can we possibly do so they will take us seriously?"

Just then, a girl who was celebrating her birthday entered carrying a huge cake, followed by another girl striking a tambourine. Everyone cheered. The *hammam* went crazy; all the girls began screaming and clapping. Were they really going to dance? It may seem like a little thing to someone who has never lived under the threat of bullets and rocks and truncheons, but for all of us, this was a huge act of defiance. In an instant, the entire *hammam* was alive with dancing and clapping, like that day in the mosque. Except here, everybody was naked.

The *hammam* walls were thick masonry. I prayed the girls' uproar wouldn't be heard outside. I began to move toward the showers. An arm grabbed my wrist. "Don't you dance, chick commander?" Sima shouted.

She dragged me to the very center of the dancing. I covered my breasts with my hands. "What kind of a commander are you? Come on! Dance!"

Sima whirled beside me. "Sima, is this really resistance?" I said, as we turned and turned together. She laughed, her dark eyes blazing. "If the Taliban find us dancing here, what do you think they will do to us, Homeira-jan?"

"They will kill us."

"So, this is our resistance!"

The following Wednesday even more girls packed into the *hammam*. "Who will begin today?" I said.

"Let me try," Sima said. She was tall; she didn't need my stool. Fresh love marks covered her neck. "We should organize a big demonstration. If we can gather one hundred or two hundred girls to stand together in front of the amir's headquarters, the whole city will know. We'll wear our burqas and demand that they reopen the schools. Does everyone agree?"

"Yes! How can we even begin to fight when our fathers and brothers won't let us out of our own houses?"

The *hammam* echoed with discussion and argument for a while and then the muttering subsided.

"Commander, will you let us dance now?" a young girl asked.

"I'm not the dancing commander," I said, smiling. "I'm only in charge of the uprising. And besides, no one has brought a tambourine this week."

One of the girls began drumming on the *hammam* metal door. The girls began to sway and spin.

Damn you all! I said to myself. *I wish you were as eager to rebel as you are to dance.*

Walking home, I asked Mushtaq, "If I decide to fight the Taliban, will you stand by me?"

Mushtaq stopped abruptly. His eyes scanned the street. "Quiet!" he hissed. "Have you lost your mind? If somebody hears, they will think we are plotters They will skin us alive and hang us on the butchers' rack." Mushtaq's face went green. "What more do you want from God? You girls sleep in every morning. Do you really think I study science or have painting classes in school these days? All I get are Arabic lessons in Qur'an and sharia . . . and the beatings."

The following Wednesday, I was late arriving at the *hammam*. Smiling, Sima pushed through the crowd to stand next to me. "Don't get angry, chick commander. These girls need to dance to relieve their frustration. Let them tire themselves out; then we can scheme together."

A while later, Sima clapped her hands for silence. "OK, girls, dancing is over. Time to begin our *jirga*, our gathering."

"So next week, let's all stand together in protest in front of the amir's headquarters."

Someone called out, "What if they shoot us?"

A deadly silence enveloped the *hammam*.

I took a deep breath. "I'm as afraid of being killed as you are," I said. "But I'm even more afraid of getting buried alive for the rest of my life without realizing my dreams."

That day, our meeting didn't end with laughter and dancing. The room was silent and gloomy when the girls showered as they murmured among themselves. Under the shower, I imagined the water was blood washing over me. Dizzy, I sat down on my stool. All of a sudden, I felt like weeping. *What have I begun?* I wondered. Sima was washing the henna from her hands. The water circling the drain was red. I closed my eyes and gathered my resolve. Finally, I stood up again on my little stool and shouted. "Next Wednesday! In front of the amir's palace!"

A cheer rang out.

"By the way," I called out, "don't come naked."

In the narrow street on the way home, that atmosphere of fear and grief within the *hammam* caught up with me. I stopped. I couldn't take another step. I fell to my knees and burst into tears. I sat crumpled against a wall, weeping. The street lay abandoned under the merciless sun, the hot wind scorching my eyes through the face mesh of my burqa. *Nanah-jan's* voice whispered in my ear, *Herat's wind spreads around hopelessness.*

"What's going on?" Mushtaq asked. "Did you have a fight with your school friends?"

I began to cry even louder.

Mushtaq took my elbow and lifted me to stand up.

I cried all the way home.

That fateful Wednesday finally dawned. I gathered up my shower pack and stool.

Madar looked up from her embroidery. "Is everything all right, Homeira?" I didn't say anything. I just gazed at her beautiful face, wondering if I would ever see her again. She had made her choice, so I had to make mine.

Mushtaq was not waiting for me outside. He wasn't supposed to. I wasn't going to risk his life.

I reached the amir's palace just before ten. I had expected to see hundreds of blue burqas darkening the plaza. There were only about ten.

How many girls had raised their hands in the *hammam*? More than two hundred.

At least I had my ten.

I reached the line of frightened girls. Under their burqas, I couldn't recognize who had come.

I said to the burqa next to me, "I'm Homeira."

The burqa replied, "Sima."

I held her hand. "Shall we do this, beautiful Sima?"

We stepped forward. The shivering line of girls stepped up right behind us. We walked up to the front gate. My heart was pounding in my chest. I heard a girl beside me weeping under her burqa.

Two Taliban walked toward us, rifles slung over their shoulders. "What do you want!" one of them shouted.

My mouth felt as dry as a desert. My tongue was glued to the roof of my mouth. I took a breath. "We want the girls' schools reopened," I said in a quavering voice.

One of the Taliban swung his head from left to right and back in indifference, looking along the line of trembling burqas. He then stared at me dismissively. He didn't get mad. He looked at our tiny group quaking in their burqas and smiled.

Another guard appeared, a senior commander. He was a tall man in a huge black turban with a black beard that covered his chest. He had a scowl that could have turned a newborn baby to stone. He raised his arm and pointed a long finger right at me.

"If you ever come here again," he said, growling like a fighting dog, "I will dig a grave for each one of you and bury you alive, right here."

Turning on his heel, he walked back toward the headquarters.

The Taliban guards laughed at us as we scattered like frightened mice. God knows why they didn't beat us to the ground; there was not a single man around to defend us.

I cried all the way home. The stool under my arm was as heavy as a tombstone. The smell of henna and halvah was whirling in my head. I cried even louder.

By the end of the week, Herat's public *hammams* had all been closed, by order of Amir Abdu-Razzaq. I never saw the bathhouse girls again. I never had the chance to tell Sima that she was my hero.

My son,

These days the gloomy sky is depressing. This morning I went for a walk in the more secluded streets behind Sunset Boulevard. There were cracks in the ground below some ancient spruce trees from where big flat mushrooms had sprouted. The mushrooms and the gray sky reminded me of the story of Baba Ghor-ghori that I heard in my childhood.

In Afghanistan, the seasonal rains begin in September or early October, at the end of autumn, and continue until the middle of March. The topography of Afghanistan is mostly high mountains, with very cold winters. According to Madar, our homeland is held hostage by those mountains. Every escape route is narrow and dangerous or impeded by heavy snow. Each spring, the rain melts the snow and the sloping valleys turn to patches of green pastures that give way to brown deserts in late summer. Our mountains are generally naked and rocky, their slopes barren of green forests.

Madar says that the soil of my homeland is full of

disappointments. Even if it rains for a year, the green quickly fades, leaving barren stones exposed.

In the countryside around Herat, after every spring rainfall and thunderstorm, thousands of mushrooms pop up from beneath the ground on the banks of streams and rivers, where the soil is softest. The areas where the mushrooms appear resemble burial grounds with the graves cast open. Madar *says that each mushroom is like a decaying woman—a woman buried alive and her name lost to memories. The largest mushrooms are the mothers surrounded by their lost daughters.*

Madar *believes that the mushrooms sprouting between sunset and sunrise are those women who are snatched away by Baba Ghor-ghori, the Roaring Papa Thunder. She says they are carried off to the sky at the close of the harvest season, when the autumn rains begin. There, hidden in the gathering clouds, Baba Ghor-ghori gnaws the flesh, but their chewed bones fall down to earth with the rain, burying themselves in the ground. And with every clap of thunder, they sprout again as mushrooms. I've always felt a special compassion for those tiny baby-girl mushrooms.*

I first heard the story of Baba Ghor-ghori on a wild autumn night when I was nine years old. On that night, the clouds were rumbling, too, and our house trembled after each sudden flash and crashing noise. I screamed in terror with every crack of thunder and cowered deeper into Madar's *arms.*

Mushtaq said, "Baba Ghor-ghori is angry again. He is

picking up his saddlebag and is on his way down to the earth to take away the girls."

Then Mushtaq stood by the window and called out, "The worst girl on earth, the most spoiled girl on earth, who always eats my share of rice as well as hers, is here. Baba Ghor-ghori, come! Take her! Eat her! Chew on her bones all night long."

I poked my head out from Madar's shawl and said, "You, Mushtaq, you are the worst. Baba Ghor-ghori will take you with him, too."

Mushtaq replied from under the blanket where he was hiding, "Baba Ghor-ghori is a man. He only takes girls. And he especially likes girls who have shining golden hair."

The thunder rumbled all night. And all night, Baba Ghor-ghori walked the streets of our city with his saddlebag over his shoulder. I asked Madar how many girls Baba Ghor-ghori had taken away with him. "You can find out from counting the mushrooms that will pop up out of the ground tomorrow morning, Homeira."

With every rainfall, Mushtaq swore that tonight was my turn. And the day following every rain he would go outside the house, searching in the alleys. He'd return, shouting, "I've found a thousand mushrooms! That means a thousand girls were taken last night by Baba Ghor-ghori. Next time, it's your turn, Homeira!"

All the girls in my motherland know that one day they will be thrown into Baba Ghor-ghori's saddlebag and disappear.

Now that I don't have you, I feel like I've fallen in

Baba Ghor-ghori's saddlebag. In his dark and compressed saddlebag that doesn't even allow me to breathe.

My little one,

I am sure you've grown big enough these days that you might venture outside to play soccer on a spring day. I want you to be careful and make sure you don't step on those mushrooms. Maybe one of those is me. I don't want to remain in this saddlebag forever. In one of these seasons, I will spring up from the ground.

8

Khoshhal

The first young man I fell in love with was Khoshhal. It seems as if at this very moment, he is smiling at me from across this room. Khoshhal was a young Talib with a high forehead, dark kohl-lined eyes, and thick black eyebrows. He had a hawkish nose and pale lips that he kept pressed together, as if preventing them from smiling. A sparse beard struggled to take root on his boyish cheeks. His long curly hair hung down to his shoulders. It swung hypnotically when he paced back and forth at the checkpoint, keeping his head low as if he were embarrassed by his good looks. His assault rifle was always slung over his shoulder.

The Taliban wore black clothes and black turbans. Khoshhal did as well, but with his youthful, handsome face, he looked like a boy. Khoshhal's black turban was faded and covered in dust. That grimy black turban is one of my saddest memories.

My attraction to Khoshhal started on the day he and the black-bearded Talib nearly caught me and my pupils dancing in the mosque. For it was Khoshhal, the young Talib, who interpreted in Dari Persian everything that his angry commander was yelling at me in Pashto. His calm presence lessened my fear. He didn't yell, he wasn't angry, in fact, he was smiling slightly. I think he knew exactly what was happening in that tent.

Later, he told me that he had been reminded that day of the wedding of his neighbor's daughter, which took place when he was a child. He told me he had danced from sunset until sunrise. And then he disarmed me with his sweet smile. He didn't speak Dari very well, but he had a captivating way of pronouncing Persian words.

I don't know what happened to me that day at the mosque. In the midst of my terror, I experienced a weird and strange new feeling. I was lost between fear and joy. I saw Khoshhal there for the first time and it took me a long while to comprehend my emotions. Every day, when I stood near the blackboard, I peeked through a gap in the curtains to the street outside the classroom where the Taliban checkpoint stood. I didn't understand at first that my heart was beating for him.

Dusk, when all the men went to the mosque for the evening prayers, was the time that I shared secretive minutes gossiping with Golchehrah, our neighbor's daughter and one of my best friends. Her tyrant brother, Wahid, never allowed her out of the house. So as soon as the men heard the *adhan* and headed toward the mosque, I would lean a ladder against the courtyard wall between our two houses, climb up, and softly call her name. Golchehrah was always waiting for me in her courtyard at dusk. If I stood on tiptoe on the highest rung of our ladder, I could peek over the wall and see her. Golchehrah never dared to climb up herself because Wahid was heartless. He'd caught her once climbing on their ladder and beaten her so badly that she was unable to move for three days. For this, Golchehrah beseeched God that all of Wahid's prayers would rebound against him and that he would burn in hell.

That day, I ran to the ladder and called out to Golchehrah, bursting to tell her my secret. As usual, Golchehrah was sad and heavyhearted. She said, "God knows how long we are going to be imprisoned in our homes because of the cursed Taliban."

I interrupted Golchehrah's lament. "Not all the Taliban are bad. You were imprisoned in your house by Wahid long before the Taliban came."

I saw her eyes widen in the lowering darkness. "Are you defending the Taliban?"

"Not *all* of them," I said.

Golchehrah raised her eyebrows with a sense of surprise. "You are wrong, Homeira, the BBC says that the Taliban are what they are. There is no such thing as a good Talib, they are all evil dogs."

"How does the BBC know what goes on in a Talib's heart?" I said.

An understanding blossomed on Golchehrah's face.

She flashed me a smile. "Aha! And now you know what goes on in their hearts? Or maybe in just one special heart?"

I felt my cheeks grow hot. "Don't make a big deal out of it, understand?" I said.

"Yes, commander."

I opened my mouth to tell her more. But with the first creak of the door opening, Golchehrah disappeared, like a rabbit diving into its hole. I giggled and cursed her brother, Wahid, in the same breath. Golchehrah and I both hated the evening prayers. They were far too short for us to gossip. The men seemed to return home again before they had even reached the mosque. I climbed down from the ladder, bursting with my secret.

After that first day of dancing, I took extra precautions to keep my students and myself safe. I kept the entrance curtains closed on both sides of the mosque, and my burqa always within reach. The students were supposed to place their Qur'ans over their notepads whenever they saw any danger. And if the Taliban entered, no one was to say anything and I would do all the talking. We had come too close to disaster once and none of us wanted it to happen again.

A week passed. As I recall, I was correcting Mastorah's homework. The class was filled with the humming sound of the girls and boys chatting together while I reviewed their written lessons.

Suddenly, Zarghuna whispered, "*Moalem Sahib, Moalem Sahib*, someone is striking the entrance curtain."

I turned toward the entrance. Someone was tapping against the heavy canvas slowly, once, twice . . . a third time. The fabric puffed inward with each soft blow. Zarghuna leaned forward toward the curtain and suddenly shouted, "*Moalem Sahib!* The Taliban! I swear to God it is the Taliban!"

My legs went weak. I almost lost my balance! I quickly threw my burqa over my head. The children scrambled to tuck their notepads under their shirts and shawls. A few of the boys stuffed their notebooks into their baggy trousers. Mastorah threw her notebook on the ground and sat down cross-legged on it with her Qur'an opened on her lap. I pressed my lips together to prevent myself from laughing.

Another louder tap struck the curtain. In the frightening silence within the tent, it sounded as loud as a rifle shot. Should I wait for the Taliban to come inside or hurry outside to confront them? My poor girls were huddling together, wing to wing, like little doves on a cold winter day.

Pulling aside the entrance curtain, I stepped halfway out. My heart stopped. A Talib was standing there, a long wooden staff in his hand. He was facing the river, with his back to the entrance to the tent. He wore a shawl, a cotton scarf, around his shoulders, covering his neck. I recognized from his profile that he was the young Talib from the week before.

"Did you want something?" I asked. Startled, he started to turn toward my voice, then stopped.

"Is that you, *Moalem Sahib*?" he asked, keeping his gaze on the river's flowing water while he spoke over his shoulder. He raised his stick in the air as if to give his hands something to do.

As much as some part of me had wanted to see him again, a terrible fear gripped my heart.

I answered, "I am teaching how to recite the Qur'an here. That blackboard is to write the verses of the Qur'an on, for those children who don't have one, so they all can see the verses. And I am always wearing my burqa inside the classroom, every day."

My words tumbled over one another in my rush to speak. He seemed to be listening very carefully to what I was saying, even though he refused to look at me.

His shawl dropped from his shoulder and I caught sight of

his rifle. Fear crawled up my ankles like a swarm of ants. My palms grew damp and sweat trickled down between my shoulder blades. I squeezed the corner of my burqa with my hand to steady myself. "Don't worry," I said. "We always leave the mosque before the *adhan*. All the girls, even the six-year-olds, are wearing hijabs. And the boys are sitting separately on the other side of the mosque, away from the girls." My tongue felt thick in my mouth. My throat was as dry as dust. "I always wear a burqa," I repeated.

The young Talib turned and faced the curtain, still not willing to look directly at me. His eyes were lined with kohl. His hair had fallen from beneath his turban, covering his forehead.

He stared at the curtain and asked in his lovely, halting accent, "*Moalem Sahib*, how can you stand being under your burqa for hours in this heat?"

I took a step back and placed my hand on my heart. "I can! I swear I can! You can send someone to check whenever you want." My voice was weak, the squeaking of a mouse. My heart shrank into a tight knot of fear.

"It must be very hard," he said. "Anyway, you could suffocate underneath that burqa." I was shocked. Wasn't he a Talib? "What are you *really* doing there in the mosque?" he asked, finally looking at me, although, in truth, all he could see was a black lump of cloth covering me completely from head to foot, with a mesh cloth hiding my eyes.

"I am teaching the Qur'an," I answered. My head reeled. I felt dizzy and leaned against the tent to steady myself. It was all over. His question wasn't a question. He knew *everything*!

The young man swung his stick slowly back and forth along the ground between us, kicking up puffs of dust. He glanced toward me again. "Yarghal, who is in your class, is from our people, from our town. I know that you are teaching literacy here, *not* the Qur'an."

I turned and glared at Yarghal. I should have known that sooner or later this loquacious *jinni* would betray our secret. Yarghal stared back at me, his face pale. A good thing he couldn't see my wrathful eyes.

I turned back to him, blocking his view of the frightened children. "What would you have me do? These kids will grow up and remain illiterate unless I teach them. They should be able to write at least their names. It's a strange world out there. God knows where destiny will send them. They should be able to write a letter to their parents and loved ones. You know that every sentence of a letter is worth half a visit."

Khoshhal turned away. He was staring silently at the river as if contemplating when to begin beating me. Finally, still looking away, he began to speak in that soft, calm voice of his. "Do you think we, the Taliban, have no parents and loved ones? Do you think no one is seeking our company? That no one is expecting our visits?" Turning, he looked directly at me. "What about us? What about me?"

He dropped his head and scraped angry furrows in the dust with the tip of his worn-out sandal.

When he looked up again, he saw that I was staring at his rifle. In a flash, he pulled his shawl back over his shoulders, covering the barrel. With that single gesture, he revealed his innocence.

My fear flew away, and I drank in his features: his long, thin face, his delicate hands, his boyish curls, and that sad, dusty black turban.

Then he looked down at his toes poking out of his battered sandals and whispered, "Can I learn here, too? Because I, too, want to write a letter to my mother."

We were living through terrible times. During those years, the Taliban forced many young girls to marry them. No one could refuse these fierce armed men, some of who were Arabs, Pakistanis, and Chechens, so daughters disappeared like smoke. This was the ugly face of religion and politics during that epoch. I was certain that *Madar* and *Agha* would have been horrified if they knew that I was thinking of teaching a Talib how to read and write.

The attraction that I felt for the Talib rested heavily on my heart. In my city, he was the enemy. But still, I wondered: *Is it the poor boy's fault that he has never had any schooling? And since there is a school near his checkpoint, why shouldn't he learn also?* I certainly felt compassion—but it was a feeling beyond compassion that drew me to him.

Two days later, I heard the same soft tapping on the mosque's entrance curtain. It was early afternoon. I was reviewing my students' homework. I put on my burqa and opened the tent flap. It was him. Pulling a sheet of paper from under his shawl, the expression on his face passed from shame and embarrassment to delight as swiftly as the shadows of clouds pass over the land. He blushed and then, finally, he smiled. Standing at arms' length, he offered me his worksheet.

"*Talib Sahib,*" I said. "What if your commander sees us?"

"*Moalem Sahib*, my name is Khoshhal."

I was stunned he would let me know his first name.

Khoshhal continued speaking. "The other day, when my commander heard clapping in the mosque, he grabbed his rifle leaning against the checkpoint wall and shouted, 'They blaspheme! They sin in the holy mosque!' He began to run toward the tent and I ran after him. When we neared the entrance, my commander started cursing and yelling '*Ḥarām! Ḥarām!* ' I chased after him, trying to calm him. 'For the sake of God, they are only children,' I said."

Khoshhal continued. "My commander entered the tent before I could stop him. I knew that you were scared; your voice from inside your burqa was like the squeaking of a tiny mouse. I saw that the children were all terrified. I didn't translate *all* the awful things he said that day, all the horrible names that he called you. He was *so* angry. And in his rage, he was blind to the pens and notebooks that *I* saw, not so well hidden, *Moalem Sahib*. You must teach children to do better.

"When we returned to the checkpoint my commander ordered me to keep an eye on you people. He said, 'By God, if they are doing anything sinful, come and tell me. I swear by the Prophet that I will set them all on fire, everyone and everything, including that shameless woman.'"

I gasped and stepped back toward the tent.

Khoshhal placed his hand on his heart. "Now, if the commander discovers that I, too, am doing something unlawful, he will burn us together."

Bending down, he placed the paper on the ground. I picked it up and, with trembling hands, I wrote out his first lesson. Was this to be the tinder that would consume us all—me, my students, and this poor young boy?

Over the next several weeks, Khoshhal came daily to the mosque's entrance to give me his homework. In that stifling tent, I waited breathlessly for the sound of his footsteps and his gentle tapping on the canvas. Placing his homework on the ground, he'd stand there gazing at the river, his face glowing with childish joy. I'd reach my arm through the curtain folds to retrieve his papers, stealing a glance at his handsome profile as he averted his blushing gaze.

Like some of the refugee children, Khoshhal was from Ghor Province to the east of Herat. He was assigned to our city for the period of his enlistment. He didn't dare befriend Heratis. And in any case, they ran away from him and the other Taliban.

"People are right to fear you and run away," I told him. "You destroyed our lives here."

Instead of becoming angry with me, Khoshhal nodded, saying, "Just a few years ago, our house was destroyed. I wasn't yet a Talib back then. I was still a small child. My older brother became a mujahid and went off to fight the Russians. He never returned. They say that the Russians murdered my brother inside a mosque. They shot him down along with all the other men. I still have nightmares: that the mosque is full of blood and my brother is drowning in the blood. For this reason, I have not been inside any mosque for many years. Now, my commander forces us to go to *this* mosque to pray five times each day. It is a torment for me."

He turned, looking right at me. "The day you were dancing

in the mosque, that was the only time since my brother's death that I wasn't afraid to set foot inside."

While I reviewed Khoshhal's homework inside the tent, he always waited patiently outside for my verdict, chewing on the tail end of his turban and shifting his rifle on his shoulder. I'd peek out after I whispered "Well done," waiting for his smile to erupt. My pulse raced as pride straightened his posture.

For every lesson, he wrote an extra page and I knew he hoped to hear my voice praising him not once, but twice.

He wrote his letters in a quivering hand, a hand that always strove to write better.

"Why does your hand shake so when you write?" I asked him.

He looked right at me. "How do you know this?"

I smiled within my burqa. "If I am the *moalem*, then I should know these things. I can tell."

Khoshhal was quiet for a moment. He scratched a line in the dirt with his sandal and said, "When my commander leaves our checkpoint, he never tells us when he'll return."

"What about your squad, won't they tell your commander about your writing?" I said.

"No," he said. "I write my lessons when I am at my guard post. Another Talib is with me, a friend. He also copies what I am writing so that he can learn as well. Our guard duty is well spent learning; otherwise, the heat and the boredom would kill us both."

I placed Khoshhal's homework on the ground. "If you like, you can bring your friend's lessons to me. I can't imagine that his handwriting is as beautiful as yours."

Khoshhal blushed. "My friend is from Helmand Province. He likes Herat very much. He is keen to quit his post and begin a life here."

"That would be a good thing," I said.

Khoshhal looked at the ground. "They won't let us do what we want. They didn't bring us here to build."

"And you think that destruction is a good way to live?"

He stared right at me. I felt he could see me blushing beneath my burqa. "So, in your mind, we were born to destroy? Have you ever seen our green pastures? Once, we had prosperous fields. But in the war, which war and under what name, I don't remember, everything was burned. It was turned to smoke and ash. If my commander allowed it, I would never leave this place. I would stay right here. I would send a letter to my mother."

When Khoshhal uttered the word "mother," I felt the pain and regret in his voice.

Shifting his rifle to his other shoulder, Khoshhal wrapped his shawl around his neck. He turned to leave. "Tomorrow, I will bring the Helmandi boy's homework to you."

I never met the boy from Helmand Province. But starting the next day, I began correcting two sheets of homework and writing *Well done* twice.

Once, I asked Khoshhal why he didn't buy a notebook. "It is too dangerous, *Moalem Sahib*. When we use sheets of paper, we can destroy them if the situation arises." Then he added, "But I never want to destroy these pages. Your name is on them beside mine."

"But that is too dangerous! I will no longer sign your homework."

"It doesn't matter. In this place we are always in danger," he whispered.

At the very beginning of their rule, the Taliban banned televisions and all books other than the Qur'an. *Agha* dug a hole in our courtyard, wrapped his books, mostly Russian literature, in sheets of plastic, and buried them in the ground. When my father wasn't looking, I stole Pushkin's *The Captain's Daughter* from the hoard that was about to be buried, secretly reading it at night under my bedcovers, using a kerosene lantern for light.

Our radio broadcast nothing except Qur'anic recitations and poems praising the Prophet. I cursed that radio every day for never announcing the reopening of the girls' schools. *Nanah-jan* warned me to repent and seek absolution for calling the radio useless. "For shame, Homeira! You are *sharor*, a naughty girl," she scolded.

Now Khoshhal brought us daily news of the war—mostly of war, only of war. Once, I asked him if there was any other news in the world. "Aren't there any other stories?"

While scuffing the ground with his toe, he said, "In the checkpoint, the commander's portable radio is the source of all our news. And, here, there is only news of the war. We are taking casualties in every part of the province. In all of Afghanistan."

"Your people are also dying," I said. "When will this horrible war end?"

Khoshhal ignored my question and continued scuffing up clouds of dust with his sandal. "They have blocked all the roads to Herat. I hope that they clear the roads soon so that I can write a letter to my mother." He lifted his head and looked at me. "I can't write well yet. Will you help me write a letter to her?"

"Yes!" I answered, that word of affirmation hanging joyfully between us.

He blushed like a small child. "We must do this soon," he continued. "There is a massive attack around the city of Mazar-e Sharif. They are sending groups of my friends to the northern front."

I bent down and placed his homework on the ground so that he could pick it up without getting nervous taking it from my hand and risking that our hands might touch. This was the law of the city that no *na-mahram*, "unrelated persons of the opposite gender," has the right to look at one another or even touch one another in the slightest. This law was born with the city and we were obliged to adhere to it.

Four days passed. When Khoshhal failed to return to the mosque, I feared the worst. Every afternoon I waited breathlessly for his long fingers to tap softly on the entrance curtain. Deep in my heart, I felt a hollow ache. *Agha* told me that the Taliban had massacred many people in Mazar-e Sharif. He said that they had been killed in the streets and in their homes. Hearing that, I was convinced that Khoshhal's commander had sent him to fight in Mazar.

Then, on the fifth day, while I was teaching in the mosque, I heard that longed-for tapping. I ran to the curtain without my burqa and flung it open. Caught off guard when he saw my face, Khoshhal spun around, facing the river. Embarrassed, I went back inside, threw my burqa over my head, and returned to the entrance.

Khoshhal looked very tired. His head hung down and his eyes were sunken deep into his hollowed cheeks. He had his scarf wrapped around his mouth. "I have been sick; I have a fever and a sore throat. My entire body is aching."

He sighed. "Every time I fall ill, I miss my mother."

"My God," I said. "I thought they had sent you to Mazar-e Sharif. I thought . . ."

He lifted his weary head and looked at me. I wished that he could see my face. "I was ill," he said. "There was no use for me at the front."

"Do you have anything good to eat? Something that will help you recover quickly?"

Staring at the ground he said, "In wartime? No soldier gets anything but war rations."

The next day I cooked some turnip soup, wrapped the pot in a cloth to keep it warm, and took it with me to the mosque. *Madar* was curious about what I was doing. I told her I was bringing soup to one of my students who was very poor and always hungry. *Madar* didn't argue with me. Even though we had very little, she knew that the plight of the refugees was much worse.

I wrote the day's exercise on the blackboard. As soon as the children began copying the lesson, Khoshhal arrived, tapping on the tent wall. I took my little pot of soup out to him. "Do you still have a fever?" I asked. He didn't answer.

"What have you brought me?" he asked.

"Soup," I said. I stooped to place the pot on the ground at his feet, in accordance with our unspoken agreement.

"No!" he said. "Don't put it on the ground. It is food, God-sent nourishment." He reached out and took the pot from me.

Khoshhal's hand was burning from fever or from embarrassment.

That evening, I could not bear the burden of my secret any longer. When the *adhan* echoed through the streets, I climbed the ladder and called my friend Golchehrah. I told her everything about Khoshhal. I told her that he was intelligent and that I thought he loved me. I told her that he hated war. Golchehrah's face turned white in the falling dusk.

The next day Khoshhal summoned me from the tent with his gentle tapping. Placing the empty pot on the ground, he looked directly at me. "Your soup was delicious. It reminded me of home. God bless your food."

Then he sat outside the tent wall and said to me, "Go ahead, ask me any word you like, and I will write it perfectly."

"Write any words you want," I said, "and I will correct them."

"You will not need to correct them, *Moalem Sahib*," he said. "They will be perfect."

Separated by that worn canvas wall, I heard his pencil scratching across the paper. And beyond that curtain, I imagined the smile spreading on his handsome face.

When he was finished, Khoshhal slid that fragile paper beneath the tent flap, waiting while I checked his work. And the first word on the page, written flawlessly, was my name, *Homeira*. His work was perfect, and I praised him. "I will return tomorrow," he said. "Then you can help me write a letter to my mother."

The next day I waited for him. And the day after. Many days passed without Khoshhal returning. Finally, I asked Yarghal to go and find him. I told Yarghal, "Please give Khoshhal regards from his *Moalem Sahib* and say that she asks about his health. Let me know tomorrow what he replies."

Yarghal didn't wait for the next day's class to report to me. That very evening, he tucked his notebook under his arm and made his way to our house. *Madar* was surprised to find him standing at our door. "What a child," she said to me as she led Yarghal into our courtyard. "His thirst for knowledge is bottomless."

Yarghal, out of the sight of *Madar*, whispered in my ear. "Khoshhal has been sent to the front." My heart froze. I sat under our mulberry tree in the courtyard in dead silence, punctuated by the occasional thumping of ripe red mulberries hitting the ground.

Five days later, *Agha* went with my two youngest brothers, Jaber and Tariq, to the public bathhouse. They returned very quickly, still unbathed. They sat on the terrace, looking very pale. *Madar* asked, "What has happened?"

Agha prepared two glasses of sweetened water for my brothers. Carrying the drinks out to them in the courtyard, he said, "The Taliban have turned the public bath into a mortuary for their dead. Many corpses have been brought back to Herat from the fighting in the northwest. They will be buried here, but first, they must bathe their dead and wrap them in shrouds."

Jaber called my name. He was six. I had been teaching him, along with the refugee children. He accompanied me when there was no other *mahram* to walk with me through the streets to the mosque tent. I went over and sat beside him in the courtyard. He was shivering, even though the day was very hot. "Yes, brother," I said.

He turned to me, wide-eyed. "Homeira! Do you remember the day we were dancing in that mosque when those two Talib came?"

I nodded, my heart gripped by fear.

"And do you remember the younger one. The tall one?"

"Yes," I whispered. "I remember."

"I saw his body there. Outside the bathhouse. He had been thrown on the ground. His eyes were wide open, and his turban was unraveled beside him, covered with dirt."

My dear Siawash,

You couldn't know it but it's true: I spend most of my nights crying in the corner of this room that has kept me so far from you.

Every day, I regret my decision to leave you. These stories I'm telling are meant to show you how strong I am, but I don't always feel strong. Nanah-jan *believes that an Afghan woman must first bear a son for the pleasure of her husband's heart and at the end a daughter for the pleasure of her own heart. She would say, without a daughter, a woman dies with a bundle of pain and suffering. I am afraid I will die with my bundle of grief and heartache.*

*My sister, Zahra, your aunt whom you've never met, and may never meet, secretly sent me a message through Mushtaq's phone that your father had sent not my whole library, but only two bags of my books to Herat. She wrote: "*Madar *and* Nanah-jan *shed tears of shame over your books." My writing is shameful in our country.*

These books haven't done anything wrong but I am afraid

my brothers will bury them as they were forced to bury all books during my childhood. And so, I am asking you, if I never see you again, I am asking you to take possession of the books at my parents' home. No matter what they may say, books are not a bundle of grief and heartache. They are the proof of my happiness and freedom. Maybe someday they will become a source of pride for you.

9

The Golden Needle Sewing Class

Of all the Taliban's many restrictions, the one that upset my family most of all might have been the prohibition against reading.

On the terrible day that the Taliban conquered Harat, *Agha* stood in front of his library, looking at his bookshelves, not saying anything. *Madar* said, "In Herat, thousands of young men are buried beneath the ground. A few books are nothing in comparison."

The Taliban were rumored to be searching every house for guns, books, and televisions. *Baba-jan* put his Hafez on top of *Agha*'s books. "We haven't survived for this long so that we die now for a bundle of papers."

That was the last time I saw *Baba-jan* reading Hafez. After dark, *Agha* wrapped his books and our small television in thick plastic and put them in an iron chest. He dug a big hole near the mulberry tree, placed the chest at the bottom, and covered it with soil. On many nights when rain lashed the ground, *Agha* stood at the window sighing, as he stared at the spot where his books were buried. Even when the garden was covered with snow, he gazed out the window, gripping his tea glass so tightly I thought it would almost shatter in his fingers.

Agha told me he had read most of his books during the war while he was guarding the trenches. "During the two days I was trapped in the mountains with Atiq, I read Pushkin's *The Captain's Daughter.*"

"*Agha*, how could you? You were reading Russian books and fighting the Russians at the same time?"

Agha smiled at me. "The people in the books are much better than people outside books. Literature is different from war."

Every year, at the end of May, when no snow remained on the ground and the spring rains were over, *Agha* made Mushtaq guard the courtyard gate so he could dig up his books. Lifting them from the iron chest, he would spread them out in the sunlight to dry.

And every year, while the Taliban ruled the world outside our walls, Zahra and I would attack those books. We would whisper the titles to each other and flip through the pages. And every year, I would beg, "Please, *Agha*, take the books and hide them in the cellar so we can read them at night."

Baba-jan always intervened. "You shouldn't take the risk. Don't bring danger into this house. We should bury the enemy under the ground."

"But *Baba-jan*, these are only books, not enemies," I said.

Baba-jan sighed. "Homeira, power defines what the enemy is. We must act prudently."

During all the years the Taliban ruled Herat, *Agha* took his books out to dry them in the sun in May. And each time, he wrapped them in thick plastic and buried them again.

The day after I read my family the first story I wrote, *Agha* dug up his books.

When *Baba-jan* saw what *Agha* was up to, he headed for the front door. "Wakil Ahmad! Don't expose this household to danger."

Smiling, *Agha* looked over at his father. "The girl who writes must read stories. I will hide the books in the cellar."

Screaming with joy, I hugged *Agha*. *Baba-jan* walked away without saying anything. *Nanah-jan* shook her *tasbeh*. "Wakil! Don't ruin your daughter's life by your own hands."

After that, at night, when all the men had returned to their homes from evening prayers and the street was empty, I read forbidden novels by lamplight. Kerosene was very expensive and difficult to find. It was imported either from Iran or Pakistan. *Madar* always complained that it was mixed with water.

Almost every night, *Agha*, Zahra, Mushtaq, and I gathered around the only lantern in the house, reading books under its smoky flickering light.

Agha encouraged me, saying, "By reading more novels, Homeira, you will become more creative. You will know more people and you will experience many different lives."

Agha was right. After I read some Russian novels, I realized that the red ants didn't just ride green tanks and wear their high boots only for war, they also danced hand in hand with their lovers in big beautiful ballrooms. They fought duels over love, and when they got drunk, they started singing.

In the books taken from the underground box, there were no burqas. There were no girls whipped with pomegranate branches and they were never traded for fighting dogs. There was no girl given away to the city's aged holy man, no beaten girl who threw herself down a well to avoid being stoned to death. There was no girl forced by her father to wear boys' clothes and to play the role of the family's son. In those buried books, women didn't whisper their stories to the water or go to graveyards to talk with the dead about their loneliness.

On so many nights, I wished that I could hide inside that hole in the yard and that somebody would bury me alive with the books. I told this to *Madar*. Smoothing her embroidered bird's half-sewn wings, she said, "They have written about their own lives. You must write about yours."

Madar didn't even look up as she was counting the stitches on the bird's wings and continued to sew.

"But, *Madar*, who is going to read my stories when we are all trapped here?"

Madar laughed and held up her embroidery. "Look at these birds, Homeira. See! We will tie your stories to the wings of these birds, and they will fly to the farthest corners of the earth."

After that, I spent all my spare time writing stories. *Nanah-jan* thought that I needed to learn how to cook. *Madar* said, "One cook should be enough in every household."

Agha was the first person who listened to my stories. He told me, "I wish there was someone who could help you with the basic rules of story writing."

Leila, Shaima, and Kolsoom were older girls that I had met at a book club in the years before the Taliban. I was very young then, so no one took me seriously. But I still went every week and sat in the corner, listening to the other girls.

After *Agha*'s comment, I decided to find these girls. I decided to look first for Leila, who I hadn't seen in the three years since the Taliban had shut our school. Leila had been an active girl, enthusiastic in school about literature and writing. *If she hasn't been married off to a Taliban commander or some other Herati man by now, she would be a big help in organizing a writing class.*

I couldn't remember where Leila's house was. I only knew it was on Baank-e Khoon Street, a long street with many lanes and alleys.

Nanah-jan overheard me. "Homeira! If you ever hope to marry a Herati man, you can't go knocking on strangers' doors. If you do, I swear that no man from here will ever propose, and if you remain unmarried, Zahra will never find a husband either. Don't dishonor your sister and yourself before everyone's eyes. You know that the walls of her house are the best witness of a girl's purity. If you are a stranger to those walls, you will have no respect in this city."

Mushtaq didn't want to be my *mahram* anymore. "Homeira, it's disgraceful and embarrassing for me to walk around the streets with my older sister. All my friends will make fun of me."

After I finished my afternoon class in the tent, I took my younger brother, Tariq, to Baank-e Khoon Street. Tariq, who was only nine, kept lagging behind. But as soon as a Talib appeared, he would huddle close to me, while I shrank against the nearest wall and tried to become invisible. I didn't know where to begin my search. I decided to ask one of the neighborhood store owners if they knew where Leila lived. I stopped in front of a bicycle repair shop, where a middle-aged man was fixing his bicycle tire. I checked that there were no Talib nearby who might see me talking to a *na-mahram*. I said hello. Surprised, the owner looked up. "Sir," I said, "I am sorry to bother you. I am looking for the house of the district supervisor."

The man looked up and down the street, then again at me. "What is his name?"

"Sir, I can't remember exactly, but I think it is Abdur-Razeq."

"What do you want from him? He is an old man, but I'm still young."

Tariq kicked the shop door with his little foot. Shaking, I took Tariq's hand and hurried away. The man's voice followed me down the street. "You didn't answer me, little chick."

The next store we came to sold fresh produce. Approaching the man sitting in front of the store, I said, "Excuse me, Uncle, where is the house of Abdur-Razeq?"

The man replied without looking at me. "See the street next to the bike shop? The first alley on your left is a dead-end alley. There are two doors in there. The green door right across from those is his house."

I slipped by the bike shop and entered the alley. There! A green door at the end of the alley. It was a very warm day. By the time I reached the green door, I was sweating beneath the burqa. I could hear noises coming from within the yard. I gently knocked. Tariq said, "Homeira! I can hear men talking inside."

"Don't worry, little brother, everyone has a brother and father, just like me."

A pleasant-looking old man with a white beard appeared at

the door. I took a step back, saying, "*Salaam*, I would like to talk to Leila if she is around."

The man looked me up and down. "Are you a sewing student?"

"No, Uncle."

"Don't stand on the street, child. Come inside the courtyard, behind the curtain where no one can see you."

As we went inside, I thought to myself: *Thank God, Leila hasn't been married off yet!*

I saw Leila coming down from the balcony wearing a white headcover. I lifted my burqa. She didn't recognize me. "*Salaam!* I am Homeira Qaderi. I was in a lower grade at Mehri Herawi High School."

Leila studied my face. "I remember you slightly."

Tariq tugged on my burqa, trying to drag me back out into the alley. "Homeira! Her father is *na-mahram*!" Pulling my little brother along with me, I stepped into Leila's house. We sat down, and Leila poured us tea. I told Leila all about my dangerous life as a secret teacher. She listened and nodded. I couldn't tell whether she was shocked or envious. She said, "You have done well, Homeira-jan. I organized a sewing class with my sister, who is an expert seamstress. We teach girls how to sew professionally."

"Leila-jan," I said, "Herat has always had tailors. Don't you think there's a need for story writers, too? My father has dug up his books from our courtyard. I am writing stories, but I need help. If you are still interested in writing stories, let's organize a writing course."

Leila said, "I have often thought about this and have tried to do something about it. The Taliban would never allow it!"

I smiled. "Leila, do you think the Taliban gave me permission to homeschool girls or to teach reading to a class of girls and boys in a mosque? The Taliban don't know what happens inside our houses. In this city, people have learned how to keep secrets."

Leila was quiet for a moment. Then she said, "I don't know any female teachers who are writers. I only know Professor Naser Rahyab."

I nodded.

Leila stared out into the courtyard. "I don't know whether my father will allow me to leave home."

I said, "If not, then the professor can come here, and I will, too."

Tariq stamped his foot. "*Baba-jan* will never allow you to!"

Glancing at Tariq, Leila said, "Naser Rahyab sells medicine at a store in the bazaar, Homeira-jan. You must also ask him for permission to let you sit in the class."

"That's fine, I'll go find him and talk to him," I said.

Tariq stamped his foot again. "Bazaar is a place only for men. You can't go there by yourself!"

Leila looked over at me. I said, "Leila, I will find him. Can you persuade your father to let us hold a two-hour class here once a week?"

Leila nodded. "Sure. My father feels bad about us being stuck at home. I think he might help us."

It was dark by the time we reached home. Both *Agha* and *Madar* were very worried. Tariq told them everything. "And tomorrow, Homeira wants to go to the bazaar!"

Nanah-jan appeared in the hallway, saying, "The girl who goes from one door to the next is no good for any door."

Agha sighed. "It will be better if I go, instead of you and Tariq."

I said, "*Agha-jan*, you are a man. Professor Rahyab can easily say no to you. He knows what the Taliban will do to us if we are caught. If I go, he might feel pity. If you go, he won't."

"So then, Homeira, what's your plan?"

"I'll write to him a detailed letter, explaining everything," I said.

That night, I wrote a long letter and revised it several times, doing my best to get the professor's attention and gain his sympathy. I wrote that I would prefer to learn story writing instead of embroidery, sewing, or carpet weaving. I promised him that we could write just as well as the men who were still active in the Herat Literary Society. The only help that we needed was advice and encouragement.

The next day, I took Tariq to Shahzadah Street. A big crowd of men was gathered in front of the bazaar. I held my burqa tightly around me. My throat was dry. I was the only woman in the street. Tariq's face was pale. Whimpering, he begged me to turn back.

Glaring at Tariq and me, the men all stepped out of my path. My knees started shaking. There was no way out. I was surrounded by their prying eyes. I kept walking until I reached the medicine market, which was filled with nests of little stores and shops. Groups of men were haggling in front of some stores. The chaos around me gradually turned to silence. No one was talking or shouting anymore; they were all looking at me. I knew no one would attack me. None of them were Taliban. But their glances were still cold and hostile. Each pair of staring eyes was a big, closed door with a sign that read: *Not one step farther!*

I just stood there, not knowing what to do. A man sitting on a chair in front of a store looked me up and down. I thought he might be a guard. I asked Tariq to speak to him. Grabbing my brother's hand, I stepped forward. I said *salaam* to the man on the chair. He growled disapprovingly calling me *"siya-sar,"* black-headed feeble girl, and said, "What are you doing here?"

"Uncle, I need to talk to Professor Naser Rahyab."

The guard scratched his beard. "I know a guy with the name Naser Rahyab from Barnabad village. You'll find him at the fourth corridor on your left."

Suddenly, a narrow path opened between the men. I looked at the guard and then at the passage lined with silent men, all staring at me. The guard glared at my eyes through the mesh of my burqa for a long while. Then, he cursed, "Damn the Devil! Isn't there a man in your household to look for that man here?"

He quickly disappeared down the first corridor. It felt like a thousand years until I saw him reappear with a young man right behind him. The bazaar was as silent as a graveyard. The man following the guard stepped up to me.

"I am Professor Monir, speak, my sister."

I said, "I have a letter for Professor Naser Rahyab."

I handed him the wrinkled and sweat-stained letter. A thousand eyes were staring at my trembling hand. He took the letter and smiled. I didn't say a word. I knew what all those men were thinking: *What a brazen little hussy to give a letter to a man.*

I turned around. The men's glances slithered under the thousand frills of my burqa. I hurried past them and reached the bazaar gate. I let go of Tariq's hand and started to run. Tariq ran after me shouting, "They are not Taliban! They are not Taliban!" But I could hear the city's voices screaming in my ears, *"Shameless girl! Shameless girl!"*

Professor Rahyab understood the danger. He knew what the Taliban would do to him if they caught him with *na-mahram* girls. But still, after our request, he agreed to teach a class every Monday afternoon.

The class was held at Leila's house under the name the Golden Needle Sewing Class. Walking to class, we all hid our notebooks beneath pieces of embroidery fabric, scissors, thread, and packages of needles.

I told Mushtaq, "I feel like a hero. I am a champion."

"No, Homeira. A hero is someone with a weapon on his shoulder, running from one mountain to another."

For the next year, we met every Monday at Leila's house, to read and discuss the stories we had written. Professor Rahyab provided valuable critique while we listened and learned.

I knew that the Herat Literary Society met every Thursday to read poems and discuss original stories—and that only men could participate. I asked Professor Rahyab, "Can we attend the men's literary society?" He laughed. "Don't ask me, Homeira. You need to get permission from the amir and from the Taliban director of Information and Culture."

A week later, the professor revealed his plan. He would take all the girls' stories to the next Thursday meeting of the Herat Literary Society, read them, and ask for the writers' comments and critique. But we could not attend.

I was overjoyed. It was enough that my new story would be read in front of an audience of accomplished writers. The men should know that Herati women were also writing stories, not just sewing and bearing children.

That night, I asked *Agha* to attend the meeting. I begged him to record all the writers' comments in a notebook, so I would know what they thought of my story.

On Thursday at three in the afternoon, *Agha* went to the Herat Literary Society meeting, and just after six he returned home, smiling. "Congratulations, Homeira," he said. "Everybody really liked your story. They have decided to publish it in Herat's newspaper, *Ettefaq-e Islam*."

I was astonished! I started prancing around the house like a week-old colt. Mushtaq sneered at me. "What? Is her story to be published? A story by an anonymous writer? No way!"

The following Monday, I asked Professor Rahyab, "Will my story be published under my name?"

He said, "No, Homeira. I hope the day comes when you can publish your own stories with your name and your picture, but I don't think we can do that now."

That same week, the Taliban beheaded the statues of all the stone horses surrounding the reflecting pool in Shahr-e Nau gardens. Herat was in shock. Herat's newspaper published articles stating that statues of living things were *ḥarām*.

It was clearly not the right time to publish my story.

A few days later, Mushtaq rushed into the house, flung off

his turban, and dipped his head into a bucket of water. When he pulled his head from the bucket, his face was pale. Looking over at me, he yelled, "I saw Maulawi Rashid enter the mosque with two Taliban. After *adhan*, he stood to pray, and everyone followed him in prayer." He was now both a Talib and a maulawi; he had both a gun and the pulpit.

Monday afternoon arrived, but I couldn't find Tariq or Jaber to accompany me to the writing group. I told *Madar* that I was late and had to leave. *Madar* threw me a worried look. "Don't take the risk, Homeira!"

"Don't worry, *Madar*, I'll only use side streets. If Tariq or Jaber shows up at home, tell them to come and find me."

I left. The street was empty. I had my burqa lifted off my face so I could see as I ran. When I reached the street across from the mosque, I froze. I couldn't believe my eyes. Maulawi Rashid was standing in front of the mosque. His beard was longer, his eyes were lined with kohl, and his baggy tunic reached below his knees. All he needed to be a perfect Talib was a gun. When Maulawi Rashid saw me, a menacing smile twisted his lips. He wouldn't take his eyes off mine. Quickly dropping my burqa, I turned onto a side street. But I could still feel Maulawi Rashid's eyes heavy on my shoulders. None of my brothers had shown up, so I took alleys where I thought no Talib would be passing by.

I had to pass by the bike shop to reach Leila's house. The owner was sitting out in front. As soon as he saw me, he said, "What are you doing here, girl? I see three of you arrive every

Monday afternoon, then a man comes. What are you doing with that man?"

I couldn't breathe. I heard the man's footsteps following me down the dead-end alley. His mocking voice whispered in my ear, "What do you girls do with that man?"

I walked faster. His footsteps quickened. I was sweating. He grabbed my burqa. His stale breath reached me through the fabric. "Girl, what is happening in there?" he hissed.

I snatched my burqa away and ran. "I will catch you! I will make you show me . . ."

I felt feverish during class. Kolsoom and Shaima had arrived before me, so I didn't know whether the bicycle man had bothered them. I was afraid to say anything; afraid that if Leila's father knew, he would say we were shaming his household and end the class. I was frightened that this tiny opening that had brightened my life would cease forever.

That day, I left with Shaima and Kolsoom so I wouldn't be accosted by the bicycle man. When I passed by his store my legs shook uncontrollably. Finally, Tariq found me. I scolded him. "Tariq, someday I will get whipped because of you."

He was a child, but he glared at me like a Talib. "*Nanah-jan* is right. Stay home. A girl out on the street deserves to be lashed."

That night, I whispered to Mushtaq, "I saw Maulawi Rashid today."

Mushtaq stared at me, then said, "Maulawi Rashid is still mad at us. Today, he came to the playground. I'd taken off my turban to play soccer. That maulawi grabbed my hair and shouted, 'Rooster! Your hair is *ḥarām*, sinner!'"

I laughed. "We punished him badly, didn't we, Mushtaq?"

Mushtaq said, "Homeira, I have a bad feeling about this. Maulawi Rashid will punish us even worse."

"So then, should we have stayed quiet?"

"No, we were in the right. But now he holds the universe in his hands."

That night, I couldn't pay attention to the book that lay open in front of me, the words melting into indecipherable black stains. Instead of being excited about going to the writing class, I began feeling guilty. *Nanah-jan* had always said that a woman shouldn't be a cause of sin for herself and others. I thought to myself, *Am I the reason for Maulawi Rashid's lust, for the bicycle man's sinful behavior?* I knew that if I had stayed at home, none of this would have happened, and on the Day of Resurrection, nobody would ask us any questions. But what if I decided never to leave the house again? Was that the right decision?

For the rest of the week, I was plagued by guilt and fear. Monday arrived, with the same problem staring me in the eyes. *Baba-jan* was too old to take me to Leila's house. Tariq and Jaber spent all their time playing and I could never find them. Khaled was only three years old, too little to be my *mahram*. I donned my burqa and left. *Nanah-jan* called out to me, "You've worn out all this city's burqas, girl."

I kicked the door and yelled, "You wore out all the world's prayer beads! What good has *that* done?"

The previous week, Professor Rahyab had promised me the Herat Literary Society would finally send my story to *Ettefaq-e Islam*. The newspaper was no longer published every day because of financial issues and the intense censoring of articles. The only articles allowed were about religion or news of Taliban casualties. Sometimes, a poem of Sa'di or a poem by a young writer was published, but only if they did not contain any forbidden words such as "wine," "lover," "dancing," or "kisses."

On Friday, as *Baba-jan* was getting ready for the noon congregational prayer and my mother was cooking, I began to work on a new story. Suddenly, I heard Tariq screaming outside.

Baba-jan and I ran out into the yard. My brother was shouting and saying, "Mushtaq was playing soccer and the Taliban arrested him."

A Talib announced to the crowd they had seen Mushtaq exchanging Ahmad Zahir's tape cassettes. As all music is *ḥarām*, they said, "He is against Islam."

One of the Taliban shouted, "Look at him! What Muslim boy wears this kind of hairstyle? What good Muslim boys listen to music? Everything this one does is *ḥarām*. We must punish these children of the Devil to teach all the others a lesson. Their heads will be shaved, we will blacken their faces, and we will make them ride donkeys around the city. That will put an end to such evil behavior."

Baba-jan was the first to apologize.

The next Monday, I had to pass Maulawi Rashid, who was standing at the top of our street. He started walking toward me. I crossed over to the riverbank, leaving the entire street to him. He crossed the street. I went in among the trees by the river. He followed me. I stopped. He stopped. There was no escape. He had his hand inside his pants between his legs, masturbating. He called out, "Every Monday, without a *mahram*, you go to see a *na-mahram*, don't you? Are you trying to bring disrepute to this neighborhood?"

I was paralyzed. I could see the knuckles of his fist beneath the fabric of his trousers as his hand stroked the swelling in his pants. He came closer, his unblinking eyes staring at my burqa-covered head. I wished a wall would appear next to my shoulder so I could lean against it. Or a tree would take root behind my back to keep me from falling. The maulawi's rancid breath surrounded me. Pushing his bulging trousers up against my burqa, he exhaled a foul question beside my ear: "Do you want to become *mahram* with me, so I will keep my mouth shut? Do you remember, my little beauty? That last time we met, I left my work unfinished? How about I finish it with you today? Your breasts are like two birds fluttering under your burqa. Do you want me to free them?"

Suddenly, the maulawi's hands were beneath my burqa, pummeling my breasts. He had glued himself to me. I didn't know where I was, in what part of the world . . . It felt as if I were being crushed between Maulawi Rashid and the tree trunk. His hand crawled from my breasts up to my mouth. I opened my mouth. He thrust two fingers inside. At that moment, I became Baba Ghor-ghori, chewing the bones of the city's men.

Maulawi Rashid screamed. I wanted him to scream so loud that his cries would be heard in hell. I clamped my teeth down on his fingers as hard as I could. He howled in pain. I hoped people would run into the street and see him pressed up against me. I bit down so hard that I thought my eyes would pop out of their sockets. Nobody came. I spit out his fingers and ran toward Leila's house.

My legs were shaking. I had to stop to compose myself. My teeth hurt, my head ached, my eyes were blinded by my tears. I hadn't taken a step into the dead-end alley when a wall crashed down on me. Panting, the bicycle man wrapped himself around me like a snake. I looked at the end of the alley, at the green door to Leila's house. The end of the alley was at the other end of the world . . . I knew that if I ran until the end of my life, I would never reach it. I collapsed to the ground. The bicycle man tried to push me onto my back, tried to force his knee between my legs. His hand was tugging at the hem of my burqa. I wrapped my burqa around my legs, holding it tight against my body so he couldn't put his hands inside. For once, my burqa was my honor.

The bicycle man hunted for my lips beneath my burqa. I wanted to chew his face off. Over and over he kissed me through the fabric, slobbering through the eye mesh, panting and grunting.

Clutching my burqa to keep his hands off my body, I couldn't fight him. I was like a trapped bird, without wings or feathers. I wished that my burqa had a thousand times more folds . . . I wished that my burqa's folds would turn into the wings of a bird to fly me far, far away . . . away from Herat . . . away from Afghanistan. I wanted to become one of those migrating birds in Afghan women's mournful songs. I wished I could turn into a water droplet and get soaked in the ground.

Hoarse, gasping breaths issued from the giant snake's foul mouth. Finally, he spat me out damp with his fetid body odor.

I sat stunned through the class, like a bird that had flown into a windowpane. Professor Rahyab looked at me and said, "Homeira, this week it's your turn to read your story."

"Homeira?"

My tongue was glued to the roof of my mouth. I looked at Professor Rahyab. My bag had fallen off my shoulder somewhere on the way to class. My story was lost in the dust of a Herat street. My book bag must've fallen as I had struggled to free myself from the grip of the bicycle repairman. I had been so distraught and distracted that I didn't notice the missing book bag.

My words had dissolved into the parched ground. My voice had disappeared down my throat. I said nothing.

Professor Rahyab furrowed his brows. "Homeira-jan, it is not easy to become a Shahrazad. You must write when it's your turn to write."

Professor Rahyab took me aside at the end of the class. "Tomorrow, your other story—the one about the bakery in Iran that would not sell bread to an Afghan refugee boy—will be published in the newspaper." I was so upset about what happened in the street that I could barely take in this good news.

It was very warm that night. *Madar* kept asking me to come up on the terrace and sleep outside with the rest of the family. But I couldn't be with anyone, even my own family. And I couldn't sleep. *Nanah-jan*'s room was always empty in the summer. I crawled into her room and cried for the entire night. Maulawi Rashid's hoarse gasps filled my ears. The foul odor of the bicycle man coiled around me like a burial shroud. The world had become an enormous wall that had collapsed on me and crushed my bones. That night, I wanted Baba Ghor-ghori to come and throw me into his saddlebag and eat my bones one by one; to grind them into dust so fine that no mushroom could ever grow from what remained. My grief was so crushing that

I hadn't told anyone that my story was going to be published the next day.

But in the morning, I had collected myself enough to tell *Agha* about the newspaper. "*Agha*, my story is going to be published today."

Everyone looked at me. *Agha* stood up, his face breaking into a smile. "Homeira, why didn't you say anything last night?"

He hurried out to find a newspaper. Tariq and Jaber ran out after him. *Agha* returned with ten newspapers under his arm. The grief of the past days had vanished from his face. His eyes were laughing. Holding out an open newspaper, he hugged me, saying, "Homeira! Look! Here!"

The words danced before my eyes: A story written by Homeira Qaderi, "The Little Man with Empty Hands." I read it again: Homeira Qaderi. My full name was there.

Smiling, Mushtaq took the newspaper, and *Baba-jan* and *Madar* each grabbed a copy.

My knees felt suddenly stronger. The scent of lilies and roses enveloped me. *Nanah-jan* took the newspaper, saying, "Where is your name, Homeira? Show me."

Mushtaq pointed at my name with his finger. For once, *Nanah-jan* was smiling. She stared at my name, then, smiling, looked at me and said, "God bless you, evil girl."

Then she touched my name.

At noon, *Agha* hurried in from the street, calling out in a faltering voice, "*Homeira! Homeira!*"

I ran into the yard. *Agha*'s face was pale. "There's a rumor that if a woman's name appears in the newspaper, she has disavowed the teachings of the Prophet. Taliban are calling for you to be whipped in public!" My father's voice broke. My legs buckled. *Madar* dropped the bowl she was carrying. It shattered into a thousand shards.

Agha turned to *Baba-jan*. "Father, would you go to the mosque to find out if this rumor is true?" *Baba-jan* stood up to leave.

Nanah-jan unrolled her prayer rug and began to pray, a corner of her hijab open to the sky.

Suddenly, a voice from the mosque's loudspeaker invaded the room. It was Maulawi Rashid. His hoarse voice stabbed my heart. "My brothers, white-bearded believers, for the past few weeks, I have witnessed a young girl from one of these houses leaving home every Monday afternoon and not returning until nightfall. Her father is just like her; he never comes to congregational prayer. Since God the Merciful forgives mistakes and faults, I won't mention the name of the family. But if this girl is seen again in the street and brings dishonor to our neighborhood, then we should ask the Taliban to teach the family a lesson."

Baba-jan returned downcast from the mosque. I was mortified for the whole family.

I crawled into *Baba-jan*'s arms and my tears fell on his turban. Wiping them away with his sash, he said, "Homeira, fighting with this hateful tribe is impossible. No story is more important than your reputation. Mansour Hallaj was a man. If he had been a woman, these vengeful people would have disgraced her in this world as well as the next. I am afraid for you. You are a girl. I am afraid of this city."

Later there was silence. No breeze rustled the mulberry leaves.

The only sounds were *Baba-jan* reciting *Surah Yaseen* and *Nanah-jan* intoning, *"Allah! Allah! Allah!"*

Agha returned home that night with a big bag on his shoulder. "I bought as many newspapers as I could. The Office of Information and Culture has ordered that every one of this edition of the newspaper must be destroyed or the sinful girl who wrote the story will be whipped in public."

My father put a few of the newspapers on the ground. Looking straight at me, he said, "We will bury these. *Inshallah*, someday the Taliban will be no more."

Then he piled the remainder of the papers in the middle of the yard and called for matches. Even *Nanah-jan* abandoned her prayer rug to come out into the yard. *Agha* threw a flaming match onto the newspapers. I stood there as silent as a corpse.

The flames flared skyward. I saw Homeira Qaderi on fire. I was burning. My eyes were burning. My hair was burning. My cheeks were burning. My heart was a candle, a torch, a beacon blazing on a distant mountaintop.

Madar threw her unfinished handkerchief into the fire: a half-sewn bird, embroidered on a patch of blue fabric. Gazing into the flames, her face veiled in tears, she said, "A wing that can't lift women's stories, our stories, into the world is no wing at all."

Dear Siawash,

My son, on the way home I was thinking to myself: What must my boy be like now? How big are his little hands? Are his lips still a chubby little bud? I asked my friend Assila who lives near your kindergarten to check on you and see how you are. But since Assila had a big confrontation with your father after the last time she tried to take a picture of you for me, she was afraid to go there. I can understand how she feels. But it is painful for me that I don't even have the right to see a picture of you. If you were to appear miraculously in front of me, would I even recognize you? If someday I were to watch you from behind a tree and you were to suddenly see me, would you recognize me?

If your father hasn't destroyed the family photo album, you could see my picture with several of my friends. In one of them, you would see me with Lida, the girl who loved to have her poetry published in Herat. But with the coming of the Taliban she became very depressed and eventually committed suicide. In another picture, you would see me with Shakiba on the day her four brothers forced her into marriage with a young man that Shakiba neither liked nor loved. I don't have any pictures of Zarghuna and Mahjabin.

None of my close friends has survived under the Taliban. Their deaths may not have made news in the world, but my memories of them live on in my daily life. We were like the seven sisters of Pleiades, a story Madar *used to tell me.*

"They are called Khosha-e Parween, the Pleiades cluster, the Atlas Sisters, or the seven divine sister stars," she said. "Originally, there were eight sisters who lived on one of the streets here on earth. One day, a warrior amir fell in love with all of the eight sisters. He ordered his troops to capture them. His soldiers did so and took the sisters to the amir.

"The amir desired the youngest sister for his first night. He told his men to make her ready for his harem. When

the sisters heard about his plans, they feared for their baby sister and asked God to turn them all into pigeons. And God accepted their wish—but only for seven of them. So while the youngest remained in the amir's prison, her sisters flew away into the sky, eventually becoming seven stars shining in the farthest corner of heaven."

10

The Girls Behind the Window

Five years had passed since the Taliban conquered Herat. They didn't mind the weather and they liked the Herati girls. Most didn't want to be transferred to another city. If assigned to posts elsewhere, they did everything possible to return to Herat. The Taliban became familiar with the surrounding villages and small hamlets where they enjoyed unchallenged authority. In time, Taliban-style haircuts and beards, kohl eyeliner, and tightly coiled turbans became a new fashion statement among Herati men. The city tailors grew skilled at sewing long, baggy trousers.

By now, the Taliban takeover of Afghanistan was almost complete and hopes of revolting against them were dashed, even as their methods became more and more aggressive. They conducted house-to-house search campaigns to confiscate hidden weapons of the mujahideen era. They broke cupboards and furniture and trampled on vegetation and gardens, searching for weapons hidden among tree branches, behind piles of firewood, and beneath the ashes of outdoor hearths. They searched chicken coops and grape arbors. If they found a gun, the owner of the house was charged with treason, beheaded, and his body hung for days in the public square like a sheep carcass.

Outwardly, we behaved like good Heratis and tried not to bring attention to ourselves. Still, danger was everywhere. One day, we were all sitting in the living room when we heard a loud knocking on the front gate. Everyone rushed out. Looking at me, *Agha* called out to *Madar*, "The women should go back inside the house. Ansari! Take your daughter to the storeroom."

I was sixteen years old and I had a woman's figure that needed to be hidden from the prying eyes of men.

Madar made me hide in a corner of the storeroom next to two large chests. One contained our school clothes—Zahra's and mine—the other was full of *Agha's* books. *Madar* covered me with two blankets.

It had been many years since the Russians and the mujahideen searched our house and my aunties had to hide. Now it was my turn. I heard the front gate open. Nobody said anything. Then the gate closed again. Crawling out from under the blankets, I looked out of the storeroom's small round windowpane stained by the muddy rain overflow. Mushtaq was outside, whispering to *Agha*. I went into the yard. "They have begun the house searches of our neighborhood starting from the first house on our block," Mushtaq said. "By now they might have reached the houses near the mosque."

Baba-jan said, "Unlatch the gate. If the Taliban kick the gate and it doesn't open, they will become suspicious and angry." *Agha* unlatched the gate and said, "Let's go inside and wait."

My uncles and *Agha* found their turbans and put them on.

A spine-chilling silence prevailed. I returned to the storeroom, ready to hide under the blankets at any moment.

Suddenly someone kicked the front gate. My heart stopped. I ran and burrowed beneath the blankets. I could hear the Taliban's loud voices. The door to the storeroom flew open. Someone was pulling up the corner of the blankets. My God! How had the Taliban found me so quickly? It was Zahra! Terrified, she crept under the blankets and began hugging me. She whispered, "I'm going to hide because the Taliban want to eat me, too."

I drew the blanket over us and hushed her. I heard the Taliban shouting at each other. I heard *Agha* saying something in Pashto. The voices in the courtyard were approaching the living room. I imagined *Baba-jan* with the Qur'an under his arm as he was the time the Russians burst into our house. I remembered a Russian kicking *Baba-jan's* Qur'an and beating him on the shoulders and chest with his rifle butt. Afterward, *Baba-jan* developed a persistent cough, but he never complained about the pain. The Taliban talked among themselves in Pashto as they searched the rooms. There was no sound of anything being broken or smashed. It was difficult to breathe under the blankets. But the fear of being found by the Taliban was far worse than suffocation. We did not hear anyone. It was dead silent. Then I heard the storeroom door open.

Zahra passed out in my arms. Silence again. *Baba-jan* was not reciting the Qur'an. A pair of legs was walking around near me. I was terrified. The crime of having books in the chest next to us was no less than the crime of hiding guns. Surely, because of those books, the Taliban would think we were infidels and kill us. I thought Zahra had stopped breathing. I heard feet walking through the rooms, kicking things. The pair of feet stopped. Then suddenly I was looking at dirty boots standing right in front of my terrified eyes alongside other covered legs, and the bare feet of *Agha* and my uncles. Raising my head, I looked at *Agha* and my uncles, standing with their hands on their heads, then I looked at two Taliban pointing their rifles at me, and finally, I looked at the Talib who had lifted the blankets where I was hiding. Shivering, I shut my eyes. The Talib said, *Allah-u Akbar*. I thought a sword was about to fall on my neck. I heard *Baba-jan* say, "For the love of God, they are both children!"

From behind my eyelids, I sensed that the other two Taliban were also looking at Zahra and me. Perhaps the sword wasn't falling after all. I opened my eyes. That Talib was still staring at me with raised eyebrows. I wrapped the long scarf around me. Then the two blankets dropped back over our heads. Darkness. I hugged my sobbing sister. She had wetted herself.

The storeroom door closed. The voices drifted out into the yard. We had been uncovered and discovered. I stood up. Zahra took my hand for comfort and security. I calmed her down. I snuck over to the dirt-stained little window. Looking out, my heart lurched. One Talib had removed the cover over the well and was looking down into it. My knees were shaking. Still holding their hands on their heads, my father's and uncles' faces had turned sallow with fear. I thought I heard someone screaming *Allah-u Akbar* in my ears. I felt like throwing up. It seemed as if the whole house was about to be bathed in blood. My vision blurred and the scene beyond the grimy window disappeared.

Moments later, I noticed *Madar* and *Nanah-jan* standing beside me, staring fearfully through that tiny window. Our minds were on this side of the window, but our hearts were on the other side. Ashen-faced, *Agha* was looking back at us from beside the well. The same Talib who pulled the blankets off me tied a rope around his waist and was lowered into the well. I wanted time to stand still even if that meant living under the tyranny of the Taliban.

Baba-jan had said that the gun he'd had for many years should have been taken away from the house, but instead, at the last minute, they had decided to bury it in our well. My God! What if they found it now? Would they assassinate *Baba-jan*? Would they murder all of us? Fear washed over me as I imagined *Baba-jan*'s white beard stained with blood again.

Someone must've exposed us. How else could the Taliban have known to go down the well?

I opened my eyes. I heard a shout. I saw the two Taliban at the edge of the well pulling up the rope. My teeth rattled with fear. My hands and feet were shaking. I gazed at the faces of *Baba-jan*, my father, uncles, and brother. That suspended moment is carved deep in my memory. Despair. During all those years of war, while our men were either on the roofs or in the trenches, our family was most fortunate because our allotment of death was small. Now, we were about to pay the price for all that good fortune.

The Talib's head appeared above the rim of the well, then his waist, and finally his empty hands. There was no rifle. Where was the rifle? The Taliban were talking among themselves. Dusting off his clothes, the Talib who had searched the well suddenly turned, staring straight at the storeroom. It was too late to pull my face away. I held my breath. The Talib began walking toward the front gate, followed by the other Taliban, with their rifles slung on their shoulders.

Seeing their backs, I dashed out of the storeroom. Our men stood stunned in silence in the courtyard. We had escaped a horrific disaster; at any moment their heads could have been put under the sword. I turned to Uncle Basheer. "Did you take the gun out of the well?" Shocked, my family turned to look at me. Everyone hissed: HUSHSHSHSHSHSH!

Mushtaq locked the gate. Numb with amazement, we all went inside. The men's turbans were still on their heads. One by one, I collected their turbans. I knew we had escaped a terrible fate . . . *Baba-jan*'s eyes were red, and I could guess that his beard was wet. *Nanah-jan* appeared with a jug of rose water. She believes that rose water has a calming effect. *Baba-jan* said, "The side of the well holding the gun must have collapsed, which made the gun fall to the bottom of the well."

"Maybe that's why the water has been muddy lately."

The next morning, *Madar* made tea and poured sugar into our glasses.

Nanah-jan said, "We must address the fact that Homeira is a woman now. It's only a matter of time until one of the Taliban comes for her."

Baba-jan nodded. "We must find a way before they burst into the house some afternoon and force us to marry her off to one of them."

Nanah-jan said, "In this land, it is better to be a stone than to be a girl."

Since the night before, I had not moved from my spot behind

the window. As they talked, for the first time I truly understood the pain of being a woman. I covered my face with my hands and cried and cried. If the glance of that Talib fell on me again and if he sharpened his teeth for me, nothing and no one would be able to stand in his way. The *nekah* would proceed according to his wishes or our home would be bathed in blood.

We knew that girls were often taken away to become Taliban wives. Our neighbor Nasreen had recently been married to a Talib who showed up at her door two nights later and said, "I've been reassigned to Khost Province. I've come for my bride."

Nasreen didn't even have time to wrap a bundle for herself. Putting on her burqa and her slippers, she stumbled out the door behind him.

I sat behind the window of our living room looking at the sky, where a cluster of stars had crept under a dark burial shroud. Must I wait for my own summons? Would I hear it tonight? Tomorrow night? I knew that if the Talib who was to be my fate came to our door, I would not allow anyone to start a war. Like Nasreen, I would put on my burqa and my slippers and I would go.

That night, in my dreams, I saw the same Talib walk onto the patio and call me by my name, Homeira! Homeira! I jumped up in fright and ran to the veranda. The Talib was standing right there like the bird Abbabil with a stone in its beak. And the named inscribed on that fatal stone was Homeira . . . The Talib pointed his gun at me, shouting, Hurry up! Then I saw myself donning my burqa, tucking my shoes under my arm, and quietly leaving the house. Then I saw myself standing on the porch with a rope around my neck. I looked at the sky. The stars were staring at me from beneath their blanket and they were crying. The Talib came and dragged me behind him.

Suddenly I saw myself in a distant place, but with that same rope around my neck and a baby girl nestled in my arms. The Talib took me to a big market where dozens of women were standing with crying babies in their arms. Every one of the women had a rope around her neck. Then I saw a man approaching. He squeezed my cheeks, saying, "Open up, open." He looked at my teeth and counted them. He told the Talib, "She is young," and then he paid him.

The new owner grabbed the end of the rope and hauled me behind him out of the market. With my baby, I am dragged through an alley that opens to a desert. The man took the baby from my arms. He noticed that it's a girl and dropped her on the ground. He continues walking toward the desert, dragging me behind him. My baby, in her newborn swaddling, was crying after me, *Madar! Madar!*

In pain and agony, I saw myself trying to run toward my baby. I saw that there were dozens of dead baby girls. Their eyes, mouths, and ears were infested with tiny worms. The man was yanking me away. I was being strangled by the rope. My eyes were bulging, and my face had turned blue. My baby was crying after me . . . *Madar* . . .

Two days after the house search, Mushtaq arrived home ashen-faced, his hands shaking. He said, "I saw Commander Moosa."

Baba-jan asked, "Who?"

"He's the Talib who climbed down our well. He was in the neighborhood with several other Taliban, asking people's names and where they lived. As I started to run away, he noticed and shouted after me in Pashto, 'We shall see the men of your household soon.' They were in a big car. A person with a rocket-propelled grenade was sitting in the backseat."

The cultural implication of his statement was clear: When a commander signaled to his men that there was a girl he wanted, they knew they were to go and get her. The system had been the same under the communists and during the civil war. Girls had no say in whom they wanted and it didn't matter who they were, what they thought, or how they looked: it was enough that they were female and had reached puberty. Besides, most of these men had three or four wives in their homes and the only real distinction among the wives was how many children they bore.

Like my friend, I knew I had no choice. If Commander Moosa knocked on my destiny's door, I would go with him without a word. My family had protected me as best they could.

That evening, *Baba-jan* wrapped his shawl around his shoulders and left the courtyard. Everyone knew where he was going, and nobody dared to say a word. A few moments later I heard knocking on the entrance to Wahid's house next door. This was followed by the barking of Wahid's fighting dogs. Then I heard Wahid's voice. Then there was silence. The sky had pulled the blanket over its daughters. Nobody went to sleep until *Baba-jan*'s return. He told us what Wahid had said: "*Haji Sahib*, we should be grateful to the Taliban that they at least come and ask for the hands of our daughters. Remember the days of the jihadis and the communists who kidnapped people's daughters and didn't honor them even with a glass of water? Commander Moosa is a young man and there is no harm in asking for your daughter's hand. He is a commander. He is an important man."

On the third day following the search, at the time of *adhan*, we heard a rumble as if a tank were crushing houses. Dust rose up in the street. A car engine roared outside the gate. Mushtaq burst into the house screaming, "They are here! They are coming!"

Baba-jan got up. My teeth began to rattle. I ran over to *Baba-jan*, saying, "If anyone gets killed because of me, I will jump into the well."

Agha ran to the front gate with Mushtaq right behind him. *Baba-jan* picked up his turban. I was searching for my burqa. *Madar* was leaning against the wall as still and motionless as any one of the adobe bricks in the wall behind her.

I was terrified that Maulawi Rashid would sneer at my family, read my matrimonial sermon, and hand me to a Talib who would take me away forever. *Nanah-jan*'s hands were trembling as she was clicking off her prayer beads faster and faster. Zahra's terrified glances swung between our frightened faces, first to *Madar*, then me, then to *Nanah-jan*. I wasn't the first in the long parade of doomed young neighborhood women who were snatched from their families and sent off to a cruel unknown fate—and I wouldn't be the last. There was no end in sight to this raging trail of terror.

I said to *Madar*, "Where is my burqa?" She looked at me blankly. In her eyes, there was no Homeira, no house, no city. The lips that should've spoken or shrieked just quivered in silence.

Suddenly the sky was filled with the chatter of migrating birds returning in V formation for the spring. My eyes were filled with their wings, my heart followed their trail through the heavens. Herat's horizon was dense with the flight of birds in a renewal of life. When I was younger, *Madar* often said, "Let's tie our wishes to the wings of the birds to carry them to a faraway land where our dreams can bloom like spring flowers."

Burqa in hand, I waited. The silence in the courtyard was shattered by someone knocking loudly on our gate. *Madar* crumpled, collapsing at the foot of the wall. *Baba-jan* came in through the front gate into the courtyard, followed by *Agha*, Uncle Naseer, Mushtaq, and Rafi Qannad, who was Nasreen's father. Commander Moosa and Maulawi Rashid were nowhere to be seen.

Nanah-jan's *tasbeh* beads were still rattling as I heard the sound of the car driving away. No one said anything. The men sat in silence. I was the bride-to-be, waiting to be swept away with my burqa. *Baba-jan* kneeled in the courtyard and dried his eyes with the sash of his turban.

Commander Moosa would have performed the *nekah* that very night, had it not been for an urgent call summoning him to Kabul. There had been an uprising in the north and the Taliban had to gather their forces. Commander Moosa had to leave suddenly, but he was planning to return. Before he left, he whispered in *Baba-jan*'s ear, "Marrying a girl will dignify her."

Baba-jan had to appear sincere and show appreciation for Commander Moosa. But we all knew it was over. Commander Moosa had set his terms. He had stolen my sleeping hours. Now he was about to own my waking hours as well.

On the fourth morning after the search, *Baba-jan* had the strength to get up on his own. When I heard his invocations of Allah, I rose from my bed. I filled his ablution pitcher. I spread his prayer rug in the direction of Mecca, and after my own ablution, I stood behind him for the morning prayer. At the final invocation of *salaam*, peace, at the end of his prayers, he looked upward, lifting the sash of his turban toward heaven. Choking on his tears, *Baba-jan* recited the prayers of gratitude. Then his shoulders began to shudder.

A week passed, during which rumors abounded that a clash had occurred between two factions of Taliban in Dowgharun, near the Iranian border. The commanders of two small factions had a skirmish and the conflict had reached higher-ups along the Taliban chain of command; guns were drawn, and several officers on each side of the conflict have been killed. One of them was Nasreen's new husband. Now Rafi Qannad wanted to go to the border to find his daughter. It was decided that Uncle Basheer would go with him.

That afternoon, *Agha*, Uncle Basheer, and Rafi Qannad left together. For two days, we had no news of their whereabouts. On the third day, in the wee hours of the night, I heard some voices. Once I was wide awake, I recognized *Agha*'s voice. I ran out of my room. *Madar* and *Nanah-jan* had reached the entrance of the hallway ahead of me. Rafi Qannad was there, standing beside my father. I wasn't wearing my head scarf. I stepped back, covering my hair with my hands. A young man in Talibani dress stood next to Rafi, and in a burst of spontaneity, I hugged him. *Nanah-jan* nearly fell down laughing, "Homeira, how dare you hug a stranger, a *na-mahram?*" *Nanah-jan* didn't know the stranger was Nasreen, disguised and dressed as a man.

Nasreen's face glowed with happiness. She could not believe that she had returned to the neighborhood. She had gone away expecting to end up in some Pakistani slave market.

I took Nasreen to the room where I, *Madar*, *Nanah-jan*, and Zahra were sleeping. We sat by the window. The moon was shining on her face.

She said, "Will it be morning soon enough so I can see my mother?"

From behind the window, I looked at the heavens. Thousands of stars had thrown away their blankets of fear and were winking at us.

When Nasreen's mother saw her in the morning at the entrance, she collapsed and Nasreen fainted in her mother's arms. *Baba-jan* leaned on the wall, letting his tears trickle into his beard.

The joy of Nasreen's miraculous return kept the dark ghost of Commander Moosa at bay for a day or two, but his looming shadow soon returned to darken my thoughts. Nasreen and I were chopping onions in our kitchen. I told her how the Taliban came to search our house and a few days later Commander Moosa returned to ask for my hand. I told Nasreen that I was ready to go with Moosa if he came back. She said, "I understand. I went with the Talib of my own accord. I couldn't take the risk of my father being harmed, not even a single hair on his head."

"What kind of men are the Taliban?" I asked.

Nasreen looked at me and said, "The first night, instead of

going to Khost, we turned around and headed for the Iranian border. We spent the night in a house with two girls from Rubat-e Sangui. That night he slept under my blanket. I accepted him since I was his wife. There was nothing I could do. I was afraid that he would pass me on to some other stranger. We girls have all heard a thousand stories.

"He did not turn me over to some other man, but you know what he did? For three nights, he strapped packages around my body and took me across the border in the dark of night. I don't know why the border guards didn't conduct a body search. Maybe no one was suspicious because I was a woman. Once I crossed the border, I was taken to Taibad; the bundles were removed and sent away. On the last night, an argument erupted over a larger package. Angry words were exchanged between the commanders. A skirmish erupted that lasted for hours. We were three girls. We waited in the house until the next morning, but none of the men returned. We climbed to the roof. We saw piles of Taliban bodies lying on top of one another in the village square. The other two girls from Rubat-e Sangui begged me to go with them. I didn't want to go. The girls left without me. The surrounding areas didn't seem safe anymore.

"On the second day, I climbed up to the roof, waiting for the crowds to leave the village square so I could escape. Suddenly, I recognized my father and your uncle. They stood in a corner of the square. Their faces were wrapped in their turbans, but I recognized my father by his cane. I ran to the village square. It was time for *adhan*. I called out 'Father dear!' My father turned toward me and said, 'Go back to the house, we'll be right behind you.'

"In the house, my father found me a set of men's clothing that must've belonged to one of the dead Taliban. I found a shawl to cover my face and a man's jacket to conceal my breasts and to cover the dried bloodstains on the shirt."

After Nasreen went home, my ears waited in fear of a knock at our front gate. My heart lurched at the sound of every passing vehicle.

By the time spring arrived with no word from Commander Moosa, *Madar* said, "The commander has not returned. I hope that soil had filled his eyes."

Madar had long said that if instead of a Talib, a Herati man asked for my hand in marriage, she would walk barefoot to Khaja Abdullah Ansari's shrine for forty Wednesdays.

And so, in the last month of summer, we heard a knock on the front gate. A neighborhood family was asking me to marry their son. *Nanah-jan* shrugged her shoulders and said, "If a mischievous girl like Homeira can have a suitor in this city, no girl will be left without a husband."

My mother was both happy and sad. "I had hoped you would be able to study. I had hoped you would write the stories of each of my broken-winged birds. But my dear daughter, at this time your safety is more important than your stories and your school. Go now! God forbid Commander Moosa suddenly appears. My only happiness is in the hope that the hundred-and-twenty-day winds of Herat blow over the heads of both of us in peace and tranquility and that you remain nearby."

Nanah-jan warned that no one should know of Commander

Moosa's proposal, as no one else would even be willing to come forward to ask for my hand. Just the name "Commander Moosa" sent chills down everyone's spines. *Madar* said, "Homeira, this is a Herati family. At least you will be close by. You won't be wandering the streets of faraway lands."

As for me, all my dreams and aspirations were dying like unwatered flowers. Wasn't there a chance that Commander Moosa would never come back, that I could escape marriage altogether? "*Madar*, I don't want to marry. Even a Herati man will keep me from my work of writing stories."

Madar put a comforting hand on my head.

"Homeira, wherever you go, make sure you take your pen with you. Just like I kept my thread and needle with me. Write in privacy. No one can take your pen or your story from you."

Nanah-jan said, "Be happy that finally you too will have a husband. You should spread his prayer rug so he can perform his prayer of gratitude."

The consensus of every family member was that it was time for me to get married.

Men came and went. *Agha, Baba-jan*, and my uncles received them and talked to them. In adherence to the traditions of our city, *Agha* and *Baba-jan* fixed the *pishkash* amount, the bridal price paid to the girl's family. Mine was a hundred million Afghanis, the same as Aunt Aziza's and my cousin's. *Nanah-jan* said, "Make sure the bride price is high so they won't think something is wrong with her."

Mushtaq said, "See how much *Nanah-jan* loves you."

It was the summer of 1997, two months after the mysterious disappearance of Commander Moosa. I was sitting behind the window in our house. My brother Tariq rushed in from the guest quarters and said, "It's all over. They gave your hand in marriage."

From behind the window in the private quarters, I saw the groom outside the guest rooms—the man who was to become my husband. Considering the large price he had paid for me, he must have been, like my brother Mushtaq, the prince of the house and the master of the street. I could only see him from the back: he was wearing a blue shirt and trousers and a gray turban, the tail end of which reached his knees. I was wishing desperately that he'd turn around so I could see his face, the size of his beard, and the color of his eyes. My father and *Baba-jan* shook hands with each of the men in the party. Mushtaq, who had hurriedly gathered the men's teacups in the living room, joined them; like other grown-ups, he pushed his way to shake hands with the groom of the family. When the groom turned around, I froze.

He looked very much like Commander Moosa. His gray turban dominated his entire forehead. He had eyes and eyebrows so black he appeared to have used a kohl eyeliner. His lips were pressed together and his long nose protruded out of his face. Like the Taliban I had seen, he was thin, but unlike most Taliban who were tall and thin, he was only of medium height.

Still, I was shocked. Why was he so strikingly similar to Commander Moosa?

I don't know how long I stood there. The courtyard had emptied and the weather had changed. I didn't want to talk to anyone. Not even my mother. I noticed that she was going back and forth between the kitchen and the other rooms. She had wrapped her face in her scarf and her eyes were red. I heard *Nanah-jan*'s voice: "Tonight, you are the bride's mother. You should be happy."

"These are not tears," *Madar* said. "They're from the smoke of the wet fire logs."

Before the week ended more men got together and there was the talk of *nekah*, the matrimonial ceremony. Once again, I was no more than a little lamb listening to all the talk from behind the door. How many people should be invited? Which maulawi should perform the betrothal ritual? What should we serve and what amount of the first installment of the bride price should the groom bring?

In the evening *Agha* informed *Madar* and *Nanah-jan*: "The *nekah* is on Monday and we will have fifty guests."

On Monday morning, I picked up the broom and swept the entire courtyard. Anger, depression, hopelessness, and fear of the man who was to become my husband were heating up every vein in my body. If I had no choice in the matter, what difference did it make whether it was Commander Moosa or this man? Neither one of them knew anything important about me as a person. What difference did it make whether I followed one man and became a refugee in Iran or married another one and ended up in Pakistan or some other part of the world? I sat in the middle of that dust cloud and wished it could become the kind of cloud that would lift me up from the courtyard and carry me in its fluff to a faraway land. I wished for King Solomon's flying carpet. What if the jinni of Aladdin's lamp was real? Once again, I felt the taste of earth on my tongue.

They decorated the men's guest quarters with plastic flowers. Before noon, my aunts arrived separately, all made up. They kissed me on the face and congratulated the men of the house with joy that another girl from the household was getting married and heading off with dignity and pride. Aunt Azizah held me in her embrace. She was pregnant and looked heavier than usual. *Nanah-jan* joyfully said, "May God always make you a boy-bearing mother."

I didn't know anything. The whole city was spinning around my head. I remembered the frogs the Russians were eating.

I felt like throwing up.

My dear Siawash,

If I knew it was you I would bear, I wouldn't have been so afraid. And I wouldn't have cried for hours that day under the mulberry tree. But at seventeen, I was afraid of experiencing the feeling of another being in my womb and I was afraid of becoming like most of the other seventeen-year-old pregnant girls in Herat. I had seen women in the city who lost their identities when they bore boys. Instead of their own names, they were called by the name of their older son: the mother of Ahmad, the mother of Mahmoud. Of course, if the first child was a girl, they would wait to give birth to a boy and then they would be referred to as the mother of that boy. My fear overtook my anger—I hope you can forgive me. I waited for years to have you because I was afraid that becoming a mother would make me lose myself, or that I would bleed to death in the process, or that I would give birth to a girl, or that your existence would prevent me from writing my stories. I am afraid I was really a woman with no strength of will and courage.

On our wedding day, the guests arrived in the afternoon. From behind the window, I was looking at the shoes that were paired up all the way to the end of the veranda. The owners of those shoes had come to announce my departure from my family with the recitation of a few verses from the Qur'an. What color were the shoes of the man with whom I would be spending the rest of my life? The dusty black shoes all looked alike. I remembered the dusty feet of Commander Moosa and his black eyes and eyebrows.

I could hear the men's conversation and their laughter. The dishes of tea and sweets were carried to the guest quarters and the men were congratulating one another in loud voices. The trail of kabob dishes followed. I could still hear the full-throated sounds of the gorging men satiating themselves. I was busy cleaning dishes in the corner of that same room when Nanah-jan *came in and said that they are about to begin the* nekah *ritual now. I was fixing my scarf on my head and shoulders when one of the men announced his arrival with the invocation of "Ya Allah." He stepped into the room and said: "I've come to ask who is the girl's representative in the matter of the* nekah.*"*

The nekah *matrimonial ceremony is the recitation of some verses in Arabic by a maulawi that, in an instant, allows a total stranger to become your master. With just a few verses,*

*a man can touch your hands, your body, and your feet. With
a few short verses recited in our guest quarters, verses that
I didn't even hear, I became the property of the groom. A
property for which the groom had paid a good price. I don't
remember what the wording of the verses was, but whatever it
was, it apparently made everyone else very happy.*

*That day I would've liked to tell them that I represent
myself, instead of my* Agha *or my* Baba-jan, *but I didn't have
the nerve. I would risk embarrassing* Baba-jan, Agha-jan, *and
my uncles. And, rebel though I was, I still felt bound by the
cultural norms of the time and place.*

Soon, Nanah-jan *spoke up: "Her representative is her*
Baba-jan, *who is the head of the household."*

*The man left without even looking at me. I would have
preferred for war to break out again, because at least then I
could go and take refuge in the underground hideout and stay
there forever. Sometimes I think I would have preferred the
crackle of bullets to the jabber of men.*

I heard them all congratulating themselves.

*It was dead silent in the women's guest quarters, where I
was awaiting my destiny with* Madar, Nanah-jan, *and my
aunts.* Madar's *face had turn limestone white.* Nanah-jan's
*lips were shivering and my aunts were keeping themselves
busy with their teacups. My fear had now been overtaken by
hopelessness. Only the* maulawi's *voice could be heard from
the men's guest quarters; he was preaching about the virtues
of marriage as if this were the Friday congregational prayer
sermon. The men were absorbing it in complete silence or
perhaps with indifference.*

Then the maulawi called: "May I ask the groom to come forward."

I could not see either the groom or the maulawi or even the rest of the people who were looking at them. I wanted a spider to appear out of nowhere in the corner of this room and spin a web around me and to gobble up the maulawi if he came toward me. Now that the edge of Madar's *scarf did not protect me, I wanted to stay within the spider's web forever. I heard the groom's voice in the other room for the first time:*

"I am the groom."

Determined and strong. Without any trembling. Happy and proud.

He was asked: "Do you accept this woman as your wife?"

He repeated his response three times: "Yes, I asked for her hand in marriage to be my bride and I am accepting her."

But nobody asked whether I wanted him and was willing to accept him.

I heard my own voice within, saying: "I am the bride."

When the groom accepted me as his bride, as an invocation of blessings in unison all the men said, Allah-u Akbar, *"God is Greater."*

Nanah-jan *took a fistful of* noqol, *the sugarcoated almonds, and ceremoniously poured them over me. I put my hand on my head as I sensed a bitter taste on my tongue. I felt a prickling on my face as if a swarm of the most vicious worms in the world were attacking my teeth and chewing my cheeks. Azizah looked at me and mumbled under her breath:*

"Congratulations, you dear one to your aunt's heart."

After the nekah, *there was a commotion as the men encouraged the groom to take a tour of the house of which he had just become a* mahram, *a lawfully permitted household member, and to see the bride alone for a moment.*

I still think of that day with fear. The groom's sister, your aunt, was telling me that the groom was very handsome and that I was fortunate. But your aunt was your father's half sister from his father's first wife and cared little for me. I felt like hiding behind my mother's skirt. Not only did your father resemble Commander Moosa, but his lifestyle was also like a Talib's. He was born in a family and culture that prized polygamy and thought women were to be bargained for with money.

"Don't be so ungrateful," Nanah-jan *said. "A man who has two wives must have the money to take care of them. In other words, if he can afford the expenses of two wives, he must be rich."*

Siawash, I did not care if he was rich. In fact, I didn't know what rich was until the day I had you.

11

Herat—Dowgharun

I don't remember the first time I really saw him up close—but it didn't really matter what I thought of him or his looks, since now that we were married, I had to behave the way my husband wanted me to behave. I had to conduct myself the way he wanted. I had to dress in whatever way he suggested. I had to cook what he liked and do whatever satisfied him. I had to follow my husband wherever he went.

Afghan tradition demands that a new couple should not live alone, and therefore must live with the husband's family. They must also live according to their household rules. My polygamous father-in-law and his two wives—known mostly as wife number one and wife number two—had left the country for Iran years earlier and we were expected to join them.

Because my husband frequently traveled across the border unrestricted, the Iranian embassy gave me an entry visa.

So, on an autumnal day when the yellowing mulberry leaves covered the courtyard, *Baba-jan* tied a loaf of bread around my waist so that I would leave for my husband's house symbolically with my own provisions. I was the last girl of my generation from our neighborhood to leave town. *Nanah-jan* hugged me and whispered in my ear:

"This man is your fortune and your destiny. Learn how to live with your fortune and destiny."

My fortune and destiny was walking several steps ahead of me. I hugged *Nanah-jan*, but the words I was trying to whisper back to her that day have clumped into a knot in my throat, even now. Mushtaq waved at me as he turned away his face so I wouldn't see his tears. In Afghanistan men don't cry. Mushtaq had become a man now.

After three and a half hours of driving from Herat through dusty trails and along a rocky road we arrived in Dowgharun, a town I had visited years earlier. This time around there was no sign of the camps welcoming refugees. This time, there was a man who until very recently was a mere stranger, and this time Dowgharun greeted me joyfully as the new bride from Herat.

At the Afghan-Iranian border, my husband stood in front of the Immigration Office and I stood behind him, as was required. The immigration clerk first checked my husband's passport and then looked him up and down carefully. Then it was my turn. My husband gave my passport to the immigration clerk. The clerk asked loudly, "The owner of the passport?" My husband said, "It is my wife's." The clerk asked even louder, "Why isn't she coming forward herself? Give the passport to her. She should approach the window herself."

My husband stepped back and handed me the passport that

the clerk had returned to him. Down deep I felt a strange kind of joy. Herself . . . Me. *Me.* I felt a sense of respect that the clerk had accorded me. I stepped forward. The clerk took the passport. He thumbed through its blank pages, which had no exit or entrance stamps on them. He then raised his head and said, "*Abji,* lift up your veil . . ." Suddenly my knees began to shake.

I lifted up my veil; I knew I was blushing. The clerk said, "Sister, raise your head."

I complied. It had been a long while since I had seen a man without a beard. He must have noticed my sudden blush. The clerk looked first at the photo and then at me. He then stamped the page and held the passport out to me. I was hesitant whether I should take the passport myself or let my husband do it. The clerk smiled; I stepped forward and picked up my passport.

My husband had fifteen brothers and sisters living in this over-crowded house, and so as often as I could I would escape to my favorite place in Tehran, Revolution Boulevard. I quickly found my way around the bookstores that sold the latest Iranian and foreign novels. I no longer had to wear the frilled burqas of Herat, so every time I could, I would wrap my head in a black scarf and head to the boulevard. This was a major step forward. At home, books, free and abundant, were a mere dream, but here in Iran, they were plentiful.

To me, Tehran was astonishingly modern in its attitudes toward women. In Tehran, almost on every street, there were swimming pools for women. Women could work; they could study.

Streets were full of cars driven by women. In rush-hour traffic congestion, women were honking angrily. For a girl from Afghanistan, this was a dream.

On the long, tree-lined boulevards, women walked side by side with men or even ahead of them—here, women did not have to walk behind their husbands. It was no longer necessary to exhaust myself looking for a *mahram* when I had to leave the house. The city was shared equally between men and women.

I would walk down Revolution Boulevard and notice all the women walking around town without male guardians. I would study them closely to get a sense of their inner state of mind. I saw boys and girls strolling, holding hands. I was astounded by their daring.

My husband's family lived on a street in Pai-Minar, an older part of the town. There was an old park near their house that was frequented by young couples. One day, I asked him if we could go to that park. I was a newlywed and I remember very well that I was wearing a green scarf with golden decorative patterns that matched my faintly visible greenish eye shadow. The whole time in the park, as we were supposed to be enjoying the lush and glorious surroundings, my husband was complaining about my eye shadow. Life might have been freer here, I thought, but still, I am expected to obey my husband. Reluctantly, I wiped off the eye shadow.

Nevertheless, in my time in Iran, I did so many things I could never have dreamed of back in Afghanistan. I joined a girls' volleyball team that played in that park in the afternoons. I wondered what *Nanah-jan* would've said if she had seen me giggling and laughing out loud with the girls and experiencing life without the Taliban and without war. In those days, life outside Afghanistan seemed exotic and sometimes unbelievable.

I was amazed to see women hurrying on the streets of Tehran with smartphones in hand. I got very excited when I saw women nonchalantly chewing gum on the street. Watching women haggle with taxi drivers or girls sitting in the park eating ice cream and discussing foreign-made hair colors: all of that shocked me! Sometimes I was intimidated by women wearing tight jeans and discussing their college majors.

The streets of Tehran were empowering and validating but they also made me nervous and angry. I wanted to be what *Madar* would have considered these women: a bad girl. I wanted to be a bad girl who colored her hair and went to college.

In Afghanistan, a good woman was defined as a good mother. In Iran, a good woman could be an independent and educated woman. I vowed to myself that I would not have a baby until after I finished my studies. By night, I was afraid and embarrassed to let my husband know that I was trying not to get pregnant, but by day, among my books and my friends, I knew I was making the right decision. If I were to get pregnant, I would be expected to remain home, and I was nervous that I would have trouble ever resuming my education.

Women in Iran were more empowered; they had fought for equal opportunity to attend university, and that thrilled me. There was so much to live for. I wanted to read novels and learn about the world. But the women at home surely wouldn't have understood. Zahra wrote to me that *Nanah-jan* had already chosen a name for my nonexistent son. Zahra would ask, "How do the women there live?"

I wrote to Zahra that there are many girls who attend Sharif University, who are very good at mathematics and want to pursue a career other than teaching. I wrote to her how this was not a segregated city, and that even the big black crows have their place strolling after the boys and girls on Wali-Asr Boulevard.

Zahra's education had been interrupted in Afghanistan. She was good at mathematics, always doing addition and subtraction on *Nanah-jan*'s prayer beads. She had written that she was hoping to become a doctor someday, but didn't see how she'd do it, now that they'd locked the school gate. I knew how frustrated she was so I didn't tell her too much about Iran because I didn't want to upset her.

But while education was easier in Iran, my husband's family was still somewhat backward: they did not believe that a girl like me, a girl who had been suppressed in the Taliban era and who had been forbidden schooling, would have the ability to study in an Iranian university. But I insisted that I could, and eventually my sister-in-law—who was always waiting for the day that I would begin throwing up in the morning—began to lose hope. She couldn't help but say, often, that a dry tree deserves to be sawed off.

The abundance of story-writing classes in Iran was one of the things that made my time there so important. I could go to class without fear of harassment by Maulawi Rashid or the bicycle repairman. I could listen to the various stories of the girls and boys who had experienced the world differently. I was living my stories and they theirs. I often did not have the courage to read my stories in front of them.

Over time, I began to tell my friends Sara and Elaheh a little about my life in Afghanistan; I still remember their awestruck looks as they closed their books and listened to my stories. At that time, no one had yet written anything about women under the Taliban. They hadn't known that such a place existed and I hadn't known that outside of Afghanistan, the world was a relative paradise for women.

Dear Siawash,

Tehran was the world of my dreams. It was there that I published the first collection of my stories. Can you believe it? Even now, many years after, I feel a little girl's joy at the mere thought of it. I was a survivor of Herat. Revolution Boulevard in Tehran redefined my life. I owe many of my joyous days to the streets of Tehran.

But that excitement would not have been possible without your father's agreement. I was luckier than most, in that I was allowed to study in his house. I know that, in some countries, getting an education is a woman's right, but from where I came, it was not. I was still an Afghan woman and was expecting to be beaten, insulted, and rebuked by society. I will never forget your father's kindness to me in this regard.

Iran was obviously a new learning environment for him. In our neighborhood women had the right to live, the right to choose, the right to laugh, and the right to scream. Both of us witnessed this together. His sisters, each one of your aunts,

married men of their own choosing and they represented
themselves in their matrimonial ceremonies.

Your father opened opportunities in my life. He saw in
me, and appreciated, the hard times I'd been through. He
looked at me with a mixture of awe and appreciation, and his
approval was reinvigorating for me. For many years, I felt like
a little girl who finally got the birthday present she wanted.

Still, he was an Afghan man, and as it is for all Afghan
men, his primary expectation of me was to bear a child. I
was stuck between trying to realize the dreams of Homeira
and satisfying the desires of your father. For a long time, I
chose the former.

Much as I love you, if I had to do it all over again, I
would still make the decision to wait until I was older and a
bit established to give birth. I never wanted to define myself
solely as the mother of children. Anyway, I felt as if my books
were my children—they were like daughters, each of whom
symbolized empowerment for women. Come to think of it now,
I don't think your father had any interest in my daughters. But
at least he never harmed me or my daughters and he didn't
punish me for them as other Afghan men might have done.

Your father and I shared life for almost fifteen years. Of
those fifteen years, there were many days when I loved him
and I followed through with every single piece of advice
Nanah-jan *had offered. I let your father walk a few steps*
ahead of me and be the master of the house. But there were
also days when I came to realize I could not, in the end,
accept him as my master. Those were the days Nanah-jan
never would have liked.

12

Revolution Boulevard, Tehran

Eventually, Tehran came to accept me as I had accepted it. At the end of the four-year bachelor program, I had grown up and told my classmates that I had a husband, even though I still didn't tell them I had been married all along. I loved my husband tremendously. It is true that ours was an arranged marriage and I was bound to him through the utterance of a few verses in Arabic whose meaning I didn't know. But with the passage of time, I grew to love and understand him, and he me.

We were tied together but we were also able to be independent.

I would go to theaters, watch movies, and learn about the way other women lived. I toured the museums and spent hours studying the remnants of the lives of people of bygone eras. I would use my daily passes for scenic bus rides through Haft-Teer Square and explore the big city of Tehran. My husband, who was studying political science at the university, preferred to lie down on the sofa and daydream. The day I received my master's degree, I went to the beauty salon and styled my long hair. Then

I stood in the doorway and said to him, "How about both of us working for our PhDs?"

I passed many an examination and, with fear and excitement, was admitted to the PhD program at Tehran University, one of the best universities in Tehran. I couldn't believe it myself. The day I received my admission letter to the doctorate program, I knelt down and cried tears of joy and triumph. Triumph over the thoughts of *Nanah-jan*. It makes me laugh when I think about the frightened little girl who blushed from ear to ear in embarrassment at the border checkpoint when she lifted her burqa for the first time.

But things don't remain in place forever. Sometimes an earthquake, a flood, or a fire comes from nowhere and washes away all the peace and tranquility you have worked for your whole life. All of a sudden, my husband wanted to return to Afghanistan. He wanted to work in the Ministry of Foreign Affairs—his dream job. He, too, had studied all these years and wanted to have power and authority. How long could he just survive as a refugee in Iran with no chance for advancement, he complained. He wanted to get politically involved in Afghanistan and work in the government. I was just a writer and all my paraphernalia was the pen I carried with me. But he wanted political power and that was available to him only in his own country.

But for me, returning to a city that fed on the blood of girls was terrifying. I was afraid the city would be the way it used to be. Cruel. I was afraid of Herat. I was afraid to go back to a place that had become a cemetery of my buried friends. I was afraid of the sudden reappearance of Commander Moosa. I was afraid that someday he would knock on the door and say, "I had drawn a circle around this girl." That secret of the past thirteen years was burning in my chest and its flames were licking my whole body. My husband was a good man, but still, I worried that, deep down, all men were the same as Commander Moosa.

Nanah-jan said, "You must keep this secret in your chest until the day you die."

I had spent half my life in the rather small city of Herat—the bitter half. Why should I return to a place where my husband had to put on kohl eyeliner and I had to wear a burqa? Herat had not progressed enough during the years of democracy, freedom of speech, and human rights to prevent female suicide in the city. The girls of Herat still had the highest self-immolation statistics in the world.

I went to Iran in a burqa and returned to Afghanistan with a few boxes of books. The sky of my homeland was blue, bullets weren't flying, and the Taliban whips weren't piercing the air. My mother's hair had all turned gray. *Nanah-jan*'s back had arched farther and *Baba-jan* had left us eight years earlier.

My husband and I settled in Kabul, which seemed at first to be a more modern city. We got a house in the Arya Housing Complex, a gated community where you were born. I established my own niche in society by working as an adviser in a ministry and a professor at the university so I could equally contribute to the family finances. *Nanah-jan* continued to be dissatisfied. Her repeated phone calls conveyed this.

"Why are you trying to become a man? Put on a floral embroidered scarf. Put on red lipstick and wait for your husband to come home at night. Men prefer women like that."

But life with my husband seemed to prove that love can exist

without red lipstick. Many of the men in the city still were trou-
bled if their wives brought in a second income; they considered
it a source of shame for their manhood. But my husband had
no problem with that. The lifestyle in Iran and the sensibility
of gender equality in that country had a positive effect on him.
The relatively forward thinking life in Iran had affected both of
us. So I was happy. I had a PhD, I had published several books
and had received several awards. I was no longer like my own
mother, who could only whisper her frustrations, but never in
my father's ear.

O Siawash, you so dear to your mother's heart,

*From those first days that you announced your presence
in my body and soul, I began telling you stories. I sang you
lullabies in the hot summers of Kabul. In the autumn, when
leaves of life fell more frequently than leaves from trees, I sang
you lullabies to block the sound of explosions. I hid you under
my shawl so you wouldn't get hurt. I had been afraid to
become a mother. But your birth showed me that motherhood
is just a different kind of womanhood.*

*Kabul is the city where they lust for power and wealth.
It didn't take much time for your father to change with the
prevailing winds there. When I bought a car so that I could
drive independently in the city and avoid the risks that taxi
passengers take on the streets, he would not allow me to drive.
He didn't show up at the unveiling of my new novel, because
he was embarrassed by the presence of other men. We weren't
in Tehran any longer; we had returned to Afghanistan, the
land that has always suppressed its women. Your father*

seemed to have returned to his roots. Shortly after that, he began preventing me from attending social and official functions. But I was no longer the seventeen-year-old naive girl who would give in to his every whim. The era of Taliban suppression was over for me.

Even though I had only one class to teach after you were born, he was treating me harshly. He pretended to be concerned about my mothering duties, but that was all a ruse to keep me in the house. I just liked to go to the university and teach; it didn't matter how many hours I taught. Being in the university environment, even for two hours, had a pleasant and calming effect on me. But your father didn't like it. Every Wednesday I went to the university, and every Wednesday afternoon he would pick a fight with me. It was Kabul, it was all a man's world.

13

Divorce, Divorce, Divorce

One day, in the summer of 2015, I was returning home from work, counting down the moments until my eyes would fall on you. On that late summer Tuesday in Kabul, I remember the sun had lowered itself so far that it almost touched the rooftop of the car that I drove so rebelliously. The wrath of thunder was threatening in the west, where dense clouds kept crawling. The wind was lifting up debris from the unswept streets and dust whirled in a rising tunnel around and above pedestrians. Scraps of paper and plastics were doing their crazy tango.

A woman holding the edge of her scarf between her teeth was struggling to keep her skirt around her body. Tree branches swayed down left and right like fearsome monsters, until the rain finally made good on its threat. The drainage system in Kabul had been messed up in the war years. Even a patchy drizzle turned the city streets into mud puddles and pedestrians were challenged to negotiate the many pools of water to find their way through the muddy maze.

In those days, I was trying not to take you out of the house unless it was absolutely necessary. I didn't want Kabul to become your graveyard, as it had been for so many.

In addition to the Taliban threats, *Da'ish*-ISIS had penetrated city streets. ISIS operatives were chopping off people's heads in back alleys while the Taliban were drenching people in bloodbaths on the main streets. Every time I returned home, I repeatedly recited all the prayers I had inherited from *Nanah-jan*. Sometimes, my white-knuckled hands would freeze on the steering wheel out of fear. I continued to drive in Kabul even though my husband didn't like that I did so. Behind the steering wheel, I was no longer a passenger in the city, I owned as much of the city as any man did.

During my work breaks, I would close my eyes and think, *What will I do when it is time for my son to go to school? Is it possible that in order to protect those beautiful eyes I will keep him within the four walls of the house?* I couldn't help but think of my poor mother, who tried to keep me in the house but I, like a stubborn spider, would do everything possible to cut the protective strings of the web she had spun around me.

By the time I got home, the rain had stopped. I opened the bedroom window a little to let the rain-washed fresh air flow in. I put the baby's red hat on him and wrapped him in an orange blanket and sat by the windowsill.

The fresh and young weeping willow branches of the Arya Housing Complex had drooped under the rain. Kabul was like an orphan in tattered clothing. Siawash was in my arms for a long time and nursed for quite a while, until he fell asleep around six o'clock, clutching my finger in his baby grasp. The minute I put him down in his bed, there was a knock on the front door. It was a friend to the two of us, a woman professor who taught at the same university as my husband. I brought her tea. She asked me to sit down and listen very carefully.

"Your husband wants to have a second wife. There is a girl in his class; she is his student. He has talked to her family. She doesn't have a father, but her brother has given his consent. When her brother and mother return from the Hajj pilgrimage, they will do the ceremony. I thought you might want to know."

She was very nervous. She didn't drink her tea but left. Well, actually, she fled.

The world sank into deep darkness. Time stood still, as if I were having an out-of-body experience. Images of the shared life of the past fifteen years were perpetually parading before my eyes.

Around nine o'clock, the key turned in the door lock. My husband was home. He took off his shoes by the door. His white socks appeared wet.

He usually turned on the TV to catch up on the latest news.

That night they were showing the ten soldiers killed and decapitated in a Taliban night raid in Farah Province.

He lowered the volume and said, "I want to share some news with you. Homeira, every land has its own specific laws. You pay no attention to the state that Kabul is in, nor do you pay any attention to my manhood. By being yourself, you call it into question."

He had accepted the whole world we had built—or so I thought. What had changed?

In Kabul I was no longer his ideal wife. I was a wife who

published books, a wife who spoke in public, a wife who came home late from teaching at the university, a wife who was recognized in her own right. A woman who behaved like this was never going to be an ideal wife to the average Afghan man.

I don't blame him. This was Kabul and not Paris, after all. Besides, one can't expect the traditional cultural norms to change in a mere fourteen years. It takes years and generations for men to accept strong women. And in the end, he felt more accountable to society than to me.

It wasn't long before we arrived at that fateful night, the night he summoned me and spoke in a portentous tone.

I may never be able to tell you exactly what happened to me then. I had heard the last part of your father's sentences as if they were echoes from a very deep well into which I was falling. I could scarcely breathe—I was suffocating. I had drowned. I was trying to call someone to get me out of the well. Only God knows how much I must have screamed. I don't remember. I don't remember at all.

It's been years since I have thought about that night, but it hangs over my head like a crumbling roof. I can barely let myself remember it, but as I sit here in California I can't help wishing that you were in my arms. I wish your father was on his way home and that I was sitting here writing stories without any worries. Yes, I still write, but I pay for these stories with your absence and I am anguished that they aren't worth losing you in the process.

But that night, you were there and you were crying and it was your crying that saved me. I went over to you. I held you in my arms and I sat on the edge of the bed and breast-fed you as I watched your father breathing comfortably in his sleep under the dim bedroom light. My eyes fell on the clock. It was two thirty. Beyond the window, the city was slumbering without apology. The big moon and star of the wedding hall neon sign were visibly blinking. Yes, the wedding hall that had stolen your father's heart. Could his needs really be that silly, and that superficial? I guess they were. He wanted a place where he would be throned as a groom for a second time.

I went to take a shower. The water ran over my hair and face and down on my breasts and stomach. I touched my belly and felts the ribbed cesarean scar under my fingers. Then I sat on the shower floor and covered my face and mouth with my hands. After several hours in the grip of shock, in the pangs of pain, and in utter disbelief, I began to cry. I cried my heart out in that unblessed morning in Kabul. I cried quietly so I wouldn't disturb your morning sleep. As for me, there was no sleep and no delusion.

Like a bird drenched in the rain and unable to fly, I had knelt on the floor of the shower. I was so drained I didn't even have the energy to turn off the water that continuously poured on my head. I wished that just once, the phoenix could rise from the ashes of Herat and fly to Kabul and bring my mother on its wings.

I looked at myself in the mirror. There were dark rings around my eyes as if someone had punched me. My lashes *had entangled and my lips were dry. Old age was staring me in the face.*

That morning, after your father left, I lay down beside you to breast-feed you. You sometimes liked to play with my hair while you were nursing . . . You would pull my hair and I would say "Ouch" and you would laugh. This time, you pulled my hair. I looked at you. You pulled my hair again and I wept bitter tears. You let my hair go and looked at me with a sense of shock.

I called my mother. In gulped sentences punctuated by frequent sobbing, I told my mother what had happened and how my tears were drenching us in sadness. There was no response from the other side.

I asked, "Mother, do you hear me?"

Her shaking voice came back. "I wish I weren't hearing this."

Again, the three of us cried . . . but Madar *could not comfort me from so far away. Those were the most painful days. I am happy that you would not remember them.*

For several days I carried the burden of my sorrow on my shoulders, alone and in silence, as I did my daily rounds between the ministry, the university, the civil rights meetings, and back home. Street by street, step by step. Nothing would take away even an ounce of my grief. Confusion and uncertainty had kept me suspended between the sky above and the earth below. The milk in my breasts was no longer enough for Siawash. My mother said, "Don't let your grief dry up your milk flow. That would leave your child hungry."

But was it even possible to overcome such grief and suffering? I had taken my womanhood over all the impassible highways and byways of the land. I took revenge from the Taliban house confinement by burying myself in books. Yet thirteen years later, the man whom I loved and with whom I had a child had turned into a Talib, whether he dressed like one or not.

Polygamy is still very common in Afghanistan, and what it requires of women is the willingness to accept that your husband has other wives, but even more, to accept that you have become just a number in the family and in the world. I would always be my husband's wife number one, but of what value is that? A number is a number and my dignity is lost.

I talked to my mother every day, sobbing loudly and telling her, "I can't, I can't share him with another and just become a number myself."

She had told me many times, "Women can share anything, but not their husbands. This is the most difficult thing they demand of the women of Afghanistan."

Siawash, I would hold you in my arms and pace the width and breadth of the bedroom. You wanted to be left alone to walk on your own, but I wanted to hold you in my arms. For all the days that I was thinking and crying, your father was busy window-shopping in the streets of Kabul, looking for stylish clothes.

It took me years to understand that the traits of a Talib cannot be measured by a person's outer appearance—his dress and garb and gear. It has been years since the black turban–donning Taliban ruled over Afghanistan, but the

Talibani mind-set is still alive and well—suppressing women every way it can. Even, or especially, your father . . .

But I knew the law of the land. I either had to do what was expected: act like other "first" wives in Afghanistan, dress nicely on your father's wedding night, cordially greet and smile at the guests, and patiently offer them tea. If I did those things, my reputation as a "good woman" would be on everyone's lips and you would be with me. Or I could become a "bad woman" and challenge the rules for my rights and the etiquette for my dignity. In which case I would lose you.

I wanted both of us to survive. I wanted to continue for my sake and for yours, my son. Not for the sake of patience, but for the sake of the higher ideal—the struggle. But what were the chances of my success in a struggle that rarely is allowed even to exist in Afghanistan? How could I succeed in a struggle that even my own Nanah-jan did not accept or believe in?

Ten nights had passed since that fateful night. He would come home joyful and happy. Sometimes when he would arrive in time, he would play with the baby. He would talk about the world outside. He would gaze at the neon sign on top of the newly built grand wedding hall.

After many days of wrangling with myself, I decided to talk to him. He had bravely and happily said what he wanted. I also had the right to say what I needed to say.

One night, I dressed in a pretty, long gown. I put on red nail polish and tucked my hair into a headband. I used some fragrant cream on my hands and waited for him to come. Around nine thirty the key turned in the lock. Before speaking, I signaled with my finger on my lips and pointed to the crib. He shook his head and took off his shoes. Surprised by my appearance, he asked, "Where are you going?"

I tried to control the shaking in my voice so I could speak authoritatively—just like he did. I said, "I also want to let you know about my decision. I never want to be wife number one."

He looked at me in shock and restrained silence. He laughed. "Well, I married you first. You are my first wife, obviously. Your math is lousy."

I ignored him and responded, "But I am no longer seventeen years old. I am not afraid of any Commander Moosa anymore. I am not happy with this arrangement. You have no right to bring another wife to this house. I don't want it. This is my house. I have worked hard for this house. I sold my jewelry to pay its down payment. I have brought my son to this world here. I am not allowing it."

His jaw dropped, but soon he glared at me and scoffed, "My right has been decided by my religion and the Prophet, not by you."

I raised my voice. "But I am not giving up my right to your religion or to the Prophet. This is my final decision. You have no right to turn me into a number."

My words were too hard for him to swallow. He choked on the response.

Anger was dripping from his eyes and mouth. His smile was insulting. For the first time in seventeen years I saw his meanness. I was terrified. I felt like he wanted to trample me with his hands and feet. I felt as if he wanted to cut my words into pieces. He took a step toward me. I knew I must have turned pale. I knew that in spite of all the preparations I had made, I couldn't hide the trembling in my voice. I realized that he knew the fear within me. But I decided not to move. When he took the second step toward me, my fear grew more.

Could my rebelliousness really result in my broken bones? Had I just threatened the courage that Kabul had granted its men? He stood face-to-face with me. My lips were quivering. I felt that even the movement of my eyeballs in their sockets was out of my control. I wanted to lean against the wall. I wanted to hold on to some firm ground. The ground was swallowing me inch by inch. He was getting taller and taller before me. I felt I was in a dungeon and that even if I could call for help a thousand times, no one would hear me. Something was screaming within me as I sank into the ground. He didn't hit me, I remember. But I had shrunk.

He exploded. "Who are you?"

The tone of his voice must've woken you up. In the midst of all my screams, I only heard your crying. I don't remember how I got out of that hole in the ground. I only remember my sobbing, which got mixed with your crying. I heard you crying. I took you in my arms and placed my nipple in your mouth.

We spent the following week in silence. The only beautiful voice heard in the house was yours.

I missed my mother. Whenever the Russian tanks would rumble outside, she would hide me under her shawl. I missed her shawl.

My only gratification was that I had stated what I wanted to say and that my bones were intact. Other than that, he had never raised his hand to me. I really owe him that he didn't beat me even when I stood up to him. It took a few hours until I got my composure back.

Saturday at ten I had a class at the university.

There were no parking spaces in front of the university. I drove around and parked on a side street. The class was on the third floor. I carried the weight of a mountain on my shoulders with every exhausting step I climbed. I felt weakness in my legs and body.

They asked, "Professor, are you all right?"

After a little pause, I responded, "Yes."

At nine thirty my phone screen lit up. It was him. "Divorce, divorce, divorce."

I held my hands on the edge of the desk. I was falling in the well. None of the students could hear my cry for help. Someone had hit me on the head again. I don't remember anything more from that moment, except the well in which I was drowning.

I knew that if a man utters the word "divorce" three times to his wife, the marriage is null and void. I couldn't believe that he would divorce me via a Viber message. Terrified and scared, I called him many times after class; he didn't pick up.

I called *Agha-jan. Nanah-jan* picked up instead.

"Homeira, listen to me for once in your life. For how long are you willing to fight the whole world? When will your sword break? Remember, this time the tip of this dagger is pointed to your own eye. If you push, it will blind you. My granddaughter, your rejection doesn't solve the problem. He is a man and will do what he wants to. His God and Prophet have permitted him. Are you fighting with him or with God?"

Sobbing, I replied, "With both of them."

Nanah-jan understood my misery, but still she said, "These traditions are the pillars of this land. If you destroy them, everything will crumble around you. They will take away your son and cause you unbearable pain and suffering. In the end, your son will legally belong to his father and you won't be able to shoulder his misery. You must accept the new marriage and your new identity because of your son."

"I will die of grief."

"Pain and grief adorn a woman," she said. "You should accept it for your own comfort. No woman's life can be compared to a man's. I swear that your eyes and ears will get used to the second wife. Don't be afraid. It is difficult for all women, but when it happens, they accept it."

The room didn't have enough oxygen for breathing. I began to cough. "*Nanah-jan*, I don't want to get used to it. He can do whatever he wants to. I have made my decision. *Nanah-jan*, this city has laws. I will go to the court and file a legal case against him. Is it even possible that they won't hear my case?"

Nanah-jan's subdued voice came through. "Oh, my God. What woman would complain about her husband!"

Once again, a heavy load piled on my heart. That night he messaged me saying that I was free to go to my father's house, but I should never forget that my son ultimately belongs to him.

He was making decisions for me after he had divorced me.

Anger and pain had filled my veins. I don't remember how long I must have stared in the mirror. Was there truth to *Nanah-jan* and her rules? After endless hours of staring at the mirror, from the deepest core of my being came a response.

NO. *Nanah-jan* and her rules were only a refuge for weak women to fall back on. It had been a long time since I had crossed what had been a red line for other women and men.

I milked my breasts in my palms and tasted it. It was bitter. The next day I went and accepted the terms of participation in the International Writing Program at the University of Iowa in the United States.

I had learned that even on a long journey, one can take only a small bag of essentials.

It's hard for me to write about the moments they took you away from me.

You were snatched out of my arms while you were asleep and placed in your father's arms. I wanted you to wake up and fight the whole city—for your sake and for mine. But you were only nineteen months old and that was too much to expect of you. When my arms were empty, I leaned against the wall. I don't remember the rest. From somewhere, I was hearing your voice calling me "Mothe, Mothe."

I had forbidden everyone from telling me about those moments that I had passed out. I only remember that when I came to, I was held by Tahmina, a friend I had met in Kabul. Everyone was there, but you weren't. Your calling voice echoed as it still often does. I hear it when the ocean washes off conic shells on the beach. I hear it when the waves hit the rocky shores, when I walk between sand castles. I hear your voice when I walk by the aloe vera spiky shoots. Just like that very first time, you kept calling me, "Mothe."

The next morning, thick patches of cloud hung so low, as if they were threatening to hit me on the head.

My dear Siawash,

Losing you was the most severe pain I have ever suffered and I know you must be very, very angry. But I felt I had to make a choice, not just for myself, but also for my country and, ultimately, for you. I don't want either of us to belong to a society that degrades women the way the Afghan society does. You, my son, are a new generation and it is my deepest hope that by the time you grow up, things will have changed—that you will become an instrument of that change.

I always have and always will want to be a mother for you, but I also need to remain Homeira for myself. I could not trade my name for a number; I could not sacrifice my freedom or my dignity. I could not become just another humiliated woman, banished to the supposed sanctuary of our home. I cannot die under a blanket as an angry, pitiful, desolate woman; I am trying to save myself and, by doing that, perhaps save other women as well.

I ask you now not only to forgive me. I know that you have suffered such pain and I am a thousand times saddened by that. But you, my child, are poised to become a man of your homeland's tomorrows. You don't have to set off on your father's path. It is my fondest wish, my son, that someday, somehow, this story I have told you about my life will help

*you and your children and your children's children create
and nurture a new Afghanistan so that the suffering of my
mother's mother, my mother, and me will not have been in
vain.*

*With the passage of time, you will grow bigger and
straight as I grow smaller and frail. But no matter the
condition, I will fight to reach you and save you. Remember,
I am not fighting just for you and me. This land has many
tight-lipped, veiled, and silenced women.*

*I will remain your storytelling Shahrazad. I will tell you so
many stories that no matter where you and I live, my stories
will reach you.*

*In my stories, no angel suddenly appears to save you
and me. In them, there is no magic wand that will bring us
together. You and I have to rise against the dark tyranny of
these monsters and fight for ourselves.*

*Come now. Let me tell you the story I promised you in the
beginning:*

*Once upon a time, there was an All-Mighty God and the
Buzak-e Qandi, which had three baby goats named Angak,
Bangak, and Kulolasangak. One day the Buzak-e Qandi went
to feed on fresh grass to sweeten her milk for her kids. But
before leaving, she warned her babies not to open the door to
any stranger.*

*A vicious wolf that has been eyeing the Buzak-e Qandi
and its kids from a distance was waiting for such an
opportunity. It came to the Buzak-e Qandi's house and
knocked on the door very gently. The kids asked, "Who's
there?" The wolf said, "Your mother." The baby goats said, "If*

you are telling the truth, show us your front hooves." The wolf ran and powdered its claws in flour and returned. It slid its powdered claws under the door. As soon as the kids opened the door, the wolf attacked them and swallowed Angak and Bangak alive. But Kulolasangak hid in the sunken oven and waited for its mother's return. When the Buzak-e Qandi came and heard the story, she was very angry. The Buzak-e Qandi went to the roof and baaed loudly: "Who ate my Angak? Who ate my Bangak?"

The wolf responded with a sense of joy and pride: "I ate your Angak. I ate your Bangak."

Buzak-e Qandi took a jug of her milk to the blacksmith and asked him to sharpen her horns. She then went to a duel with the wolf. The wolf attacked the goat with its sharp teeth. The goat ripped the wolf's stomach with its sharp horns and rescued her babies, joyous and smiling, from the wolf's stomach. Then, with the help of the baby goats, she put a heavy stone in the wolf's stomach so it could move no more.

My baby, I miss you. I have cried for you so many times. But I have never lost hope. I know that one day, we will, together, take our stories to the bazaar and free thousands of beautiful babies.

I know that you've been told I am dead. But I am not dead, my dear Siawash. I am very much alive.

I am your mother. My name is Homeira. And this is my voice.

Acknowledgments

This book would not have been possible without the friendship of many who enriched my life, empowered my struggle, and inspired me to soar: The childhood playmates with whom I collected spent bullets as toys between every lull in the fighting; the neighbor girls with whom I shared life's sad stories on the ladders we placed against the shared wall between our compounds—stories that could only be written in the twinkling stars.

I am grateful to the beautiful refugee children from the surrounding provinces who brought their innocence, their simplicity, their love, and their stories to our neighborhood in Herat so that I could homeschool them in my mother's kitchen, away from the watchful eye of the Taliban patrol.

I owe much to the young girls of Herat, many of whom fought for their rights and for their lives. Some became martyrs, succumbing to patriarchal order; others are still fighting for gender equality, social justice, and civil rights. From early on, I saw myself in many of them as we followed parallel paths, resisting tyranny through cultural, literary, and artistic expression.

I would like to thank my entire family—immediate and extended—who are the cast of characters in this memoir. They appear on the pages of this drama, as they are, "warts and all."

The greatest gratitude and appreciation must go to my parents, who raised me, along with my siblings, under the most dire and challenging circumstances. To my mother, who modeled through mothering, inspired through wisdom, and guided me through the maze of impossibilities. To my father, who taught me literature and introduced me to the world of poetry and literary writing. I owe it to *Baba-jan* on whose turban edge I dried my tears many times and whom I miss every day. To my *Nanah-jan*, who still tries to bring me within the fold of her rules—submission to the unquestionable laws of men.

I also want to offer my appreciation to the many friends in the United States who were there for me during the most challenging times in my personal life—friends, relatives, and even strangers who filled the space around me when the nest I had woven with love had unraveled: Sima Amiri, Mahbuba Temori, Mary Mayel, Hamidullah Zazai, and many others whose names could easily fill half of these pages. I would like to thank Zahra Sepehr, my wonderful friend and attorney, who is pursuing Siawash's custody case in the courts in Kabul.

I am indebted beyond words to my good friend James Prier, who suggested that I write the book as a memoir rather than as a novel. James salvaged my writing as he reviewed and commented on the first draft many times. James saw this book as his "baby." His keen eye even zeroed in on a chapter title that eventually became the name of this memoir. I am greatly thankful to him and to his wife, Shelley Mason, who believed in what James and I had undertaken. I thank them both for their indulgence, for their patience, and for their advice.

I am also grateful to my good friend Vanisa Saffari, who was eager to translate some of the early chapters of this memoir. She was able to patiently render the pained voice in my story into English. I thank my friend Brian Glyn Williams and his friend Deborah Rodriguez, whose acquaintance led me to my literary agent, Marly Rusoff.

I want to thank Marly Rusoff, who took the time to read the first draft and who was able to see that the rebel in this narrative has a cause she is fighting for—giving voice to the silenced struggle of the women of Afghanistan and of the third world.

I appreciate the efforts of Sara Nelson and her dedicated colleagues, Jane Cavolina and Jennifer Teng, at HarperCollins who did their due diligence in editing and revising the memoir, making sure the final product landed safely on bookstore shelves.

I owe particular thanks to Dr. Zaman Stanizai, whose cross-cultural understanding of both the American and the Afghan societies helped bridge the gap between them. I am grateful to him for being ready and willing to take over midway the task of translation and editing of this memoir and for reading patiently through the many drafts of translations and revisions.

Last and certainly not least, I am deeply indebted to my son Siawash for being in my life. His presence led me to fight for the principles of womanhood and motherhood. If it hadn't been for the strength of our bonding, I would probably have never experienced the longing Afghan women experience when they go through custody battles without any moral or legal support. Siawash has taught me that mothering in Afghanistan often amounts to running on the sharp edge of a sword.

About the Author

Homeira Qaderi is an award-winning Afghan writer and a courageous advocate for women's rights and the empowerment of Afghan civil society. Born in Kabul, she spent her early childhood in Herat during the Russian occupation. For a time as a child, Homeira lived the harsh reality of a refugee life under a tent in an Iranian village across the border.

She returned to Afghanistan in the calm before the storm of the civil war. She lived her teen years under Taliban suppression, but she didn't give up on her activism. She was one of three girls who secretly pursued literary writing. Homeira wrote short stories and had them published under her name. She secretly taught the internally displaced children in refugee tents and in her modest home in Herat. She was witness to the self-immolation of her best friends. These suicides left deep scars on Homeira. In her teen years, she gave in to a marriage proposal and headed for Iran once again.

In Iran, Homeira became even more determined to write her own destiny. She pursued her advanced studies at the university.

While studying in Iran, for five years Homeira served as director of the Afghan Artists and Cultural Instructors Society.

In the meantime, Homeira began writing novels in earnest. In 2003, she received the Sadegh Hedayat award in Iran for her short story titled *"Baz Baran Agar Mibarid,"* "If It Is Going to Rain Again." She also published the following books:

> *Anis' Earring*, a collection of short stories, 2007.
>
> *Noqrah, a Girl from Kabul River*, a novel, 2009.
>
> *100 Years of Story Writing in Afghanistan*, nonfiction, 2009.
>
> *The Painting of a Deer Hunt: A Fable of Women and Men*, a novel, 2010.
>
> *Aqlema*, a novel, 2015.
>
> *Reflection of War and Exile in Stories of Afghanistan*, nonfiction, 2015.

Homeira obtained a bachelor's degree in Persian literature from Shahid Beheshti University in Tehran in 2005. In 2007, she received her master's degree in literature from Allameh Tabataba'i University in Tehran and was admitted to the PhD program in Persian literature. In 2014, she was awarded a PhD in Persian literature by Jawaharlal Nehru University in India.

After returning to Afghanistan, Dr. Qaderi began her career as a professor of Persian literature at some of the most renowned private universities in Kabul, such as Mash'al, Gharjistan, and Kateb. During the same period, she became an active member of the civil rights movement, focusing on ways to achieve equal rights for Afghan women.

In 2011, Dr. Qaderi presented in the UN-sponsored Second Bonn Conference in Germany: The International Conference on

Afghanistan on the plight of Afghan women and their fight for equal rights. In the same year, she presented in China on alleviating poverty and promoting better conditions for women in Afghanistan and on the deprivation and oppression of Afghan women.

In 2012, Dr. Qaderi attended the Tokyo Conference on Afghanistan, organized by 100 countries and their civic activists. As a member of the Afghan delegation, she requested that foreign assistance to the Afghan government be directed to benefit Afghan women. In December 2014, Dr. Qaderi participated in the London Conference on Afghanistan.

Dr. Qaderi also worked as an adviser to the minister of labor and social affairs. She worked within the government system to improve the dire conditions of widows and orphans and tried to establish programs so that they would be able to achieve self-sufficiency.

In 2015, Dr. Qaderi was invited to attend the International Writing Program at the University of Iowa. She was then invited to present on the plight of Afghan women in several cultural forums in California, where she took up residence.

After returning to Afghanistan in December 2018, Dr. Qaderi accepted an appointment as a senior adviser to the minister of education with the government of Afghanistan. In that capacity, she traveled extensively in Afghanistan to see educational facilities and opportunities for women in the provinces.

There is no one more capable or more well positioned than Homeira Qaderi to provide readers with an intimate, personal, and riveting chronicle of one defiant girl's coming of age in a war-torn Afghanistan. In her own words:

As one of the youngest refugees the Soviet-occupied Afghanistan of the 1980s produced, I breathed in resilience in the cradle. The day I was caught in the crossfire on the way home from the bakery could've been my last; instead, I made it home safe—not so the loaf of bread whose edges were bitten off by a very hungry child—the teeth bites were my size by a mere coincidence. The day my aunt Zahra was martyred before my eyes could've been my last or the day my aunt Azizah, who was walking just one step ahead of me, when a bullet struck her in the knee, knocking her to the ground. Kismet could've written it as my last day when I fell from the motorcycle and smashed my face on a rock as we were being smuggled across the border or the day my little brother Jahid was run over by a trailer truck as we both tried to cross the street. My last day in this world could've been the day the Taliban poured into our house searching for hidden weapons and Commander Moosa's eyes fell on me instead, or any day during the three years I spent in exile after my baby was snatched from me—I could've died in any of those moments I was away from my son. . . . And there were many other days when several of my close friends died by self-immolation. I died with every one of them, but my spirit always rose from the ashes. I just couldn't die so soon; not if the battle for women's rights in Afghanistan was still raging where the injustices were too severe, the suppression too intolerable, the task too daunting, and the risks too high. The chick commander had to rise to the occasion and listen to the drumbeat of a forward march as destiny watched from the nearby hilltops.